KING

KING

"Times like these require a King"

KEVIN J. HIGH

Published by

CYTATION L.L.C.
CHARLESTON, SOUTH CAROLINA

Cytation LLC
227 Rutledge Avenue, Charleston, SC 29403
Visit our Web site at www.cytation.com

First Edition: October 2012

King: Times like these require a King

Includes bibliographical references and index.

Library of Congress Control Number: 2012917017
Cytation Press, Charleston, SC

ISBN-13: 978-0615698113 (Cytation Press)
ISBN-10: 0615698115

Book cover designed by Joseph Hall
Printed in the United States of America

For the amazing support of my kids, family and friends.

CONTENTS

CONTENTS

PART THREE: New Executive Departments

List of Charts

CONTENTS

KING

Why I Must Be King?

You can try and change the world by showing everyone a better way
But the world's gonna do what the world's gonna do at the end of the day
State your peace, go ahead and say it, I swear it can't get much worse
Make your peace with history, a blessing from a curse
State your peace; blow it wide open, did you find you an oyster pearl
Make your peace with history; you just might be the one who can change the world.
Hootie & the Blowfish, State Your Peace.

About six years ago, my son and I were discussing a CNBC news segment about Congress. As I saw it, Americans suffered while Congress slowed progress with their partisan debates. I complained to him that nothing will ever be accomplished because the Congressmen were too focused on ensuring their own political and financial growth. I went on to explain the frustration that I felt because the country's emphasis on obtaining power rather than encouraging progress is breaking the United States' federal government.

"Dad," my son stopped my rant, "what would you do to change things?"

I replied, "I'd need to be King for a couple of years."

Since that conversation, my ideas to change the country have percolated around this thought of being King to seek out and fix the issues in the federal government. I believe in democracy, but a strong hand is needed to repair America's broken federal system. Perpetuating certain problems in our government may not be criminal, but only because those who make the laws have kept it from being so. As I will lay out in this book, several policies in place right now exist for the benefit of our leaders to the detriment of us, the people (who are also their employers). If there is one thesis of this entire book, it is a single sentence out of which I've gotten loads of traction over the years: if you take the money out of the crime, the crime goes away.

But who can we trust to make sure this happens? Not the people who have created the system and who have kept it on life support all these years. We could vote them out of office, but anybody who has kept their thumb to the pulse of politics for the last few decades knows that our other options at the polls are no more likely to end the cycle of political self-interest. Maybe some are willing, but not nearly as many as we'd need to have hopes that congress would vote through any of the alterations that we need. The change must come by temporarily giving someone beholden to the people exclusively, rather than to the political system, the power to set things right. This is the King I envision for America.

So if America needs a King, what do I think she needs a King to do? First, though I am a dedicated student of politics, I'm sure there are many problems and corruptions that have escaped my notice. While fixing the problems of which I'm aware, I will appoint a team of experts to seek out as many new problems as possible. This team will be comprised of experts in fields relevant to their charge with no political careers to safeguard. This will keep them focused on the troubles plaguing most Americans instead of the interests of particular groups. They will be businessmen, economists, scientists, etc. These experts will collaborate with me to come up with a plan to tackle whatever new problems turn up if those problems are not already addressed by the strategies laid out later in this book.

This will be the beginning of my four-year Kingdom to ensure the long-term growth and sustainability of the United States of America. If you're reading this book, you're obviously invested in trying to figure out how our government can be improved. It is my hope that you will agree with me that, whether implemented by a king or by a congress, that the ideas that follow should have been executed yesterday.

My Kingdom will not eliminate democracy; rather it will encourage the development of the free market and the entrepreneurial spirit. There will be many goals for my kingdom beyond the effort to eliminate corruption. Without pressure from interest groups and with only the improved lives of Americans in mind, I will make specific changes to the economy. As has happened since Colonial times, innovation from businesses and entrepreneurs will continue to drive the American economy, creating opportunity for small businesses and the Americans they will employ. This will be the first step toward rejuvenating these failing markets, which will be the start of allowing America to grow out of its current economic problems.

During my four-year reign, I will implement many of the changes mentioned in this book and changes using analyses made by experts who will be striving to do what's best for American. These experts will try to change the core foundation of the problems—these will not be reactionary changes brought on by political polemics.

Partisans from either side of the political spectrum will undoubtedly find points of contention throughout this book. Those holding the mindset so popular on Capitol Hill that either Republicans are wrong so Democrats won't do it, or that Democrats are wrong so Republicans won't do it, may find their loyalty tested by ideas that challenge those generally held by their party. However, it is my hope that those disgruntled feelings will swiftly give way to our shared interest in doing what makes the most sense, and that we will all demand better from our parties of choice. You can also take heart that while my changes will sometimes be displeasing to both parties, they will also include approaches that incorporate ideas from both the right and the left – but only when those ideas cater to increased well-being for all

Americans. One example that should be pleasing to everyone is how I will consolidate, eliminate, and revamp departments and select agencies. After reviewing the appropriate literature and analyzing the responsibilities of these government organizations, I have developed a plan about what needs to eliminate wasteful spending, but also to keep what works and to make it more efficient. Whatever our political differences, efficiency in government is some common ground we should already share. From there, we can make this journey together.

INTRODUCTION

INTRODUCTION

King of the United States

I do solemnly swear that I will faithfully execute the office of President of the United States, and will to the best of my ability, preserve, protect and defend the Constitution of the United States.

Oath of Office for President of the United States

I am fed up with the politics of Washington DC. As Americans, we have heard this sentiment vented in many venues: on the news, on the radio, in the newspaper, at dinner parties, and more. I have decided to switch from stewing in frustration to taking action by making lasting reform to these broken systems that have persisted in the United States. I will bring the country back on course by becoming the King of the United States.

During my four years of service to the United States, I will sniff out the country's biggest problems with the goal of resolving the crimes in our broken political bureaucracies. As King, I will assemble a royal cabinet with the express assignment of finding and changing wasteful, ineffective, or out-of-date laws, policies, agencies, and departments. My cabinet members will work to stop these financial and political crimes, which will allow what is best for the nation to unfold free from the corruption of political posturing. My changes will enrich the local communities and empower free enterprise, putting America back on track to being one of the most powerful countries committed to rewarding all of its hard-working citizens with the rights, liberties, and access to the benefits of free-market growth. Free enterprise does not include too big to fail monopolistic companies. As King I will encourage companies to grow to that size and to then require them to be good corporate citizens.

Give Government Back to the Community

In a letter to William Stephens Smith in 1787, Thomas Jefferson wrote:

> What country has ever existed a century and a half without a rebellion? And what country can preserve its liberties if their rulers are not warned…that their people preserve the spirit of resistance…The tree of liberty must be refreshed from time to time with the blood of patriots and tyrants.[i]

I believe that Thomas Jefferson meant that each generation must pressure its leaders to modernize systems of governance based on contemporary socio-economic and political situations. We need a sweeping change of the government because the current methods of serving as a politician is sucking the vigor out of America's tree of liberty and, by extension, preventing our government from adapting to what's needed to thrive in the current global economy. Sadly, the cost of that safety net is a system that is very slow to get things done, which has caused it to slip further behind the times with every generation, preventing our government from adapting to what's needed to thrive in the current global economy. It's time to refresh our systems to reflect an economy based on e-commerce and fast-moving change. I am by no means proposing a bloody revolution. Rather, the solutions that I present throughout this book are simple and reformative and based on the axiom that if we take the money out of the crime, the crime goes away. Change is hard and uncomfortable but it is necessary and we have gotten to the point where it is necessary *fast*! There will be winners and losers. In this case the winner is the American Dream.

Under my rule, the federal government will give less funding to fewer programs. This retraction of "big government" will allow communities to come up with plans that address their particular state and local needs for issues like energy, education, and health and human services. My Kingdom and royal cabinet members will issue and take away federal block grants based on the success of these community programs. Further, social issues like abortion, prostitution, legalization of marijuana, and gay rights just to name a few, will all be locally mandated and no longer under the jurisdiction of the federal government.

During my four-year reign, the solutions to community problems will be explored, implemented, and modified by state and regional authorities. This community-based localization of power puts the government back in the hands of the United States citizens and local leaders, enabling them to empower their communities. For example, I will stop the concentration of farming in one particular area of the country by contributing federal funds to programs focused on developing community supported farm systems. In this way, should the food supply be damaged, the entire country will not suffer mass-starvation. Additionally this will create millions of jobs, reduce energy consumption and bring back life to the communities involved. Monoculture as we fund it today is an example of an ineffective federal program.

As King, I will enact and instill change that reduces the number of programs that fall under the direct responsibility of the federal government. I will pass seven royal amendments that will considerably change the federal mandate: change the requirements and term-limits for politicians, change politicians' compensation, change how districts are formed and implement line-item veto power. In addition, I will establish an interstate insurance board and an oversight department responsible for ensuring sustained and continued reorganization of community development. Under the new system, all federal taxes will be replaced by a national consumption tax and the revenue from this tax will pay our liens, military expenses, construction projects, and energy programs.

During my reorganization of the government, there will still be many governmental programs that will need to remain federalized, but many established federal programs will be reframed: interstate infrastructure and construction, centralized military protection, and regulated emissions and power standards. This is because construction and infrastructure projects need federal funding to regulate across interstate boundaries. Infrastructure also includes the technology of the federal government, which I will address with the establishment of a new federal office. Another responsibility of the federal government will be consumer protection and employee safety standards, such as those established by the Occupational Safety and Health Administration (OSHA). Like infrastructure projects and safety standards, pollution standards and nuclear power regulations need to be standardized at the federal level in order to ensure the safety of our power grid. Because the primary role of the federal government will be to protect the country from an attack, my Kingdom will be responsible for coordinating missions, regulating equipment, and standardizing requirements of the military.

In short, by limiting the number of programs the federal government has direct responsibility for, the power to rule their communities will be given back to the people of the United States.

Free Enterprise

Free Enterprise is fundamental to whom we believe we are as a people.
Our system is not primarily about money but about freedom and flourishing. The questions we face are cultural, not financial. And politicians, Republicans or Democrats, meddle with our culture of free enterprise at their peril.[ii]

Arthur C. Brooks, The Battle

Free enterprise has stood as the backbone of the American economy since before the thirteen colonies consolidated into one nation and it has served us well. Still, we should never get complacent and should always be on the lookout for ways to improve it. For instance, free enterprise suffers when we go to war—and we have been at war with Afghanistan since 2001. The spirit of entrepreneurialism is lost because war/conflict allows the government to create programs that inspire nationalism, unity, and collaboration.

While this is important to focus on nationalism during wartime, left unchecked this can lead to the reduction of civil rights. Perhaps the most clear cut example in our history are the numerous individual liberties put to the chopping block by the U.S.A. PATRIOT Act. This type of industrial focus during wartime is necessary to ensure that we have everyone behind the mission of the country, but as King I will ensure that nationalism cannot ever again be used to subvert individual liberty.

While people might argue that our current economic plight is a difficult time to evoke the rugged individualism of an entrepreneur, I think that free enterprise is the best way to allow for resurgence of the worldwide economy. When the government is given too much control over the market, free enterprise is devalued. When we live in an era of overregulation, the economy suffers because overregulation does not allow for growth, creativity, and regeneration.

Adam Smith's 19th century Laissez faire approach to the economy is not one that would work in modern day America. I'm not calling for the total elimination of the federal regulatory systems; good oversight and regulation is needed. But I am calling for reform. I'm calling for us to try to make things better instead of becoming content with the way they are. For example, the Occupational Safety and Health Administration (OSHA) is an example of good regulation. There is no argument that OSHA's officials do a very good job with ensuring safe work environments for Americans by doing things like placing limitations on the age of people who can work and number of hours per week people are allowed to work.

Parts Two and Three of my book will further expound on instances when the federal government will have direct responsibility for a program or service.

Finland exemplifies a government that fostered an economic environment of free enterprise growth. In the 1990s, Finland's banks collapsed and their economy went into a recession. Their recession has been attributed largely to overregulation of their economy. This cause for the collapse became even more apparent when Finnish authorities attempted early deregulation during the fall of the country's economy. They were successful with deregulation only after the failure had naturally run its course. And now, the country is a success story for the concept of deregulating business.

Free enterprise can occasionally get a bad rap. That rap usually stems from "too big to fail" companies. Those companies in my Kingdom will have to live with much higher standards. However, small and large businesses that do things the right way will immerse themselves in their communities and will reap the benefits of doing so. They will enrich and enliven their local economies by hiring employees and maintaining commerce in their areas.

Royal Amendments

On day one as King, even before my first cup of coffee, I will enact seven royal amendments that address what I see as the core problems in the political and taxation systems of the United States. While I explore these changes at greater length in Chapters One and Two, the next couple pages should cover the basics of what I intend to do. The first five amendments relate to how the leaders of the government will obtain power and how that power will be managed. The remaining two will modify the tax code.

Let's start with the five royal amendments dealing with how governing the power of our leaders and prospective leaders. First, I will modify the term limits for presidents, senators, and congressmen to allow them more time to get familiar with the intricacies of their role as a legislator. I want to set them up to succeed.

Next, I will make it necessary for people to resign from any other public office when running for a different position office. The nation can ill-afford to pay legislators to run the country while they are on the campaign trail. An example would be when President Obama was a Senator and running for President. Under my royal amendments he would have had to resign first and take the risk of not winning instead of knowing he still has that Senatorial job.

Another change would be making it mandatory to serve as governor of a state, before serving as president of the United States. Running a governmental body is a complex task, requiring knowledge of economics, diplomacy, science, and a host of other disciplines. We need to be sure that we're putting someone in office who has had to learn these things already and who has demonstrated mastery of them by successfully running a state. There's a lot to do as the leader of the free world, and the less time the President must spend learning, the better.

The Fifth Amendment relates to pay for our Federal Elected officials and their executive staff. Each Congressman's pay scale must mirror the average income within his respective district. By earning what their average constituents make, Congressmen will understand how to come up with programs relevant to the financial needs of their district, rather than simply voting for a raise for themselves. On top of that, members of congress will be unable to receive entitlements that aren't also offered to our military officers. Federal healthcare, retirement benefits, and other perks must be the same as those received by our servicemen and women. If the services and benefits are good enough for the military, they will be good enough for Congress.

Finally creating a clear formula on how political districts are created and changed. District lines should be drawn to balance the load on our leaders, not to afford a particular party a political advantage.

The first five royal amendments will alleviate what I see as overwhelming federal election and financial stressors. These stressors have led to public frustration as the reason many of them exist is undoubtedly to allow public officials to put their hands deep into the cookie jar by manipulating the system. By eliminating these stressors, the politicians will be able to focus on doing their jobs well. When politicians do their jobs well, they are doing what's best for the country.

I believe the most important restructuring amendment will implement the line item veto, allowing the president to override sections of legislation without rejecting the entire bill. This line-item veto will allow the president to act like the CEO of the United States, holding him or her directly accountable for the final approval of the bills. With the stroke of a pen the President will be able to render countless hours of effort by lobbyists and special interest groups from hiding earmarks in a bill. While the President of the United States will not be allowed to add or change the wording in the bill, he will be able to red-line parts that he doesn't believe should be passed. After he eliminates the parts that he doesn't like, he may then pass the bill into law. The oversight for this new power will remain: a 2/3s majority in the house and senate can overrule and override the president's decision, thus maintaining the system of checks and balances that lies at the very heart of democracy's success.

The last two amendments are the subject of Chapter Two and they will address issues related to taxes and the budget. The balanced budget amendment will ensure that America is put on a plan to substantially reduce if not eradicate the national debt by 2045. I will also use an amendment to establish the consumption tax system. This system based on the products that Americans buy will annul the income-based tax system. The balanced budget amendment and the consumption tax system will improve the failing financial systems that are currently holding the United States back from fully emerging as a free-market, free-enterprise, powerful-world player on the stage of commerce and industry.

As all of the tax loop-holes will be eliminated, this system will ensure that everyone is treated the same when it comes to taxes. Everybody will be taxed when they purchase luxury items, such as a dinner at a nice restaurant, and not taxed on necessities like groceries. This part of my royal plan will allow the United States to be self-sufficient, self-managed, and self-perpetuating. It's our country. As we fix it financially, every year it will belong less to our creditors and more to us.

The remaining parts of the book focus on my royal modifications to the Executive Branch. Each chapter in Parts Two and Three of this book will explore the changes that I will make to this branch of government's departments and relevant agencies. I will tap into the ideas of current business, political, and academic leaders to help solve the problems perpetuated by each of these government departments. By being the King of the United States, I will not be bound by red tape and will actually be able to implement the changes. My royal cabinet will be composed of the following leaders: T. Boone Pickens

(Energy); Arthur Brooks (Treasury); Lynn Tilton (Defense); Brigadier General Judge James Cullen (Justice); Brent Scowcroft (State); Jack Welch (Labor); Peter Thiel (Homeland); Malone Mitchell, III (Community Development & Sustainability); and David Camp (Consolidation, Coordination, & Ethics). For each department, the chapters in Parts Two and Three will present broad overviews of responsibilities, what works and what needs improvement, and solutions the royal cabinet and I will implement to fix the relevant problems.

While Part Two covers already existing departments, Part Three explores my royal government's two new departments and the reasoning behind their creation. To set the stage for the two new departments, Chapter Nine focuses on the modifications of the Department of Homeland Security. This chapter briefly examines what has worked and what has failed in the creation of the first executive department established in the Twenty-First Century. In Chapter Ten, I discuss the creation of the Department of Community Development & Sustainability (CDS). This department will determine which community programs receive block-grants in relationship to health and human services, agriculture, education, arts and humanities. The CDS will become an oversight agency for former health, welfare and human services programs

I describe another new department in Chapter Eleven. The Department of Consolidation, Coordination, & Ethics (DOC) will have the primary responsibility of managing the changes implemented during my reign. The agencies and offices within the DOC will serve an inspector general-role for other departments and agencies. Members of this department will ensure that my plan stays in place and that my plan is adjusted to address the needs of the changing times. The DOC will house a new agency that addresses technology in the federal government. The Technology Commission will have a three-fold mission: make all federal platforms compatible, standardize all websites for easy consistent navigation by the American people, and promote transparency of non-classified information. The main goal of the DOC will be to ensure that the representatives of the federal government continue doing what is best for the United States.

In every facet of the federal government, I will make changes that will take the money out of the crime and make a stronger, more unified United States. To do this we will eliminate wasteful spending, ineffective programs, and over-regulation. Also, we will get rid of the political maneuvering that has become necessary to make change in the United States. In my four year Kingdom, every politician will put their partisanship aside to take a long-term approach to deciding what is best for the United States. With the restructuring amendments, the country will no longer be ruled by election timelines, rather officials will seek out ways to do what will be good for the U.S.—what will stand the test of time. Through a sustained effort, the new federal government will be able to own America by making the country debt-free. Throughout my reign, my aim is to work with my royal cabinet to take the money out of the crimes in federal government by implementing my federal restructuring and budgeting amendments and by revamping the federal government's departments and agencies.

KING

ROYAL AMENDMENTS TO THE CONSTITUTION OF THE UNITED STATES

Royal Amendments

Royal Amendment One: *The President shall be given the power of the Line-Item Veto. Said veto power will make it constitutional to delete sections of proposed bills without having to return said bill to Congress for re-approval. Further, all lobbyists must fully disclose all of their interactions with politicians.*

Royal Amendment Two: *Federal Officials shall not hold an elected position while running for a different office and all federal officials must wait two years prior to accepting non-government positions related to their work while in the government. Prior to running for President, candidates must have been a governor of one of the United States.*

Royal Amendment Three: *Federal districts must be within a box based on longitude and latitude of the earth. That box must be consistent in size within each state or a states county.*

Royal Amendment Four: *Each term for the President and Senators shall be six years. Each term for members of Congress shall be four years. The terms of the President and Senators will be limited to two apiece and Congressmen will be allotted three terms. These terms may be consecutive or non-consecutive.*

Royal Amendment Five: *The President shall be paid no more than six times the median income of the entire United States. Members of Congress and Senators shall be paid no more than 3.5 times the median income of their district. In the event that Congress is unable to approve a federal budget, all elected officials forfeit all parts of their compensation until Congress approves aforementioned budget. Further, no compensation, of any kind, may be accrued during the time there is not an approved budget. Benefits for politicians will be the same as the benefits offered to the members of the military.*

Royal Amendment Six: *The Consumption tax shall be used to collect a twelve percent (12%) tax on all non-life-essential purchases in the United States. The Sixteenth Amendment will be repealed to delete all existing federal income taxes.*

Royal Amendment Seven: *Ten percent (10%) of the consumption tax collected shall be applied to paying down the national debt. Once the debt is at a zero-balance, ten percent (10%) of the collected consumption tax shall be placed into an Emergency Relief Fund set aside for domestic emergencies until the fund reaches five percent (5%) of the total GDP.*

KING

PART ONE:

New Government

And

Taxes

One: New Government

On August 11, 1997, President Clinton signed that year's Balanced Budget Act into law. As with any budget, he had to weigh his options carefully. However, that year he had a new executive privilege that allowed him to shorten the deliberation between the Executive and the Legislative branches. Rather than prolonging the debates and potentially causing a shut-down of the government, Clinton decided to use the line-item veto to override sections of the bill before signing the Balance Budget Amendment of 1997 into law. He agreed with all but three parts of the Congressional budget. Without sending the bill back to Congress for approval, Clinton struck these three provisions, and the budget of 1997-1998 was signed and approved.

Clinton had Speaker of the House, Newt Gingrich, to thank for this new authority. Traditionally, the Constitution's Presentment Clause had given the President authority to approve either all or no part of any bill presented to him by Congress. As part of his "Contract with America," Newt Gingrich amended this mandate when he ushered the Line Item Veto Act of 1996 through Congress. This federal law gave the president power to override certain sections of proposed legislation. This was instantaneously controversial as soon as Clinton used the line-item veto to delete a provision related to Medicaid distribution in New York State. The controversy: the medical employees (doctors, administrators, etc.) who were affected by the presidential line-item veto had claimed the president had inflicted a personal injury on their livelihood with his new power. As such, they decided to sue Clinton. The case made it to the Supreme Court in 1998. The President used the line-item veto several times before the Supreme Court deemed the act unconstitutional in a 6-3 decision.[iii] The court's reasoning? The line-item veto violates the Presentment Clause of the Constitution, requiring that the President reject or accept all or no part of the bill. That decision marked the end of the brief era of the line-item veto. I believe the Supreme Court was correct in striking down the Line Item Veto Act of 1996 because it is in fact prohibited by the Constitution. The Justices were right in their decision that the Constitutional precedent with the Presentment Clause prevented the legality of the Line Item Veto Act. As such, I believe it is now time to amend the Constitution to allow for the line-item veto to be legalized. By allowing for the line-item veto, the bill-making process will enter the Twentieth Century.

***

Prior to serving as the country's forty-second president, Clinton was the governor of Arkansas. He is joined in this qualification by several other marquee presidents, namely, Jefferson, Johnson, Theodore and Franklin Roosevelt, Reagan, and George W. Bush. With these presidents, whether in agreement with their politics or not, the country was well-managed by these experienced executives who were once chiefs of their home states. I compare it to being a head of a department before becoming the head of an entire company. Consider the example of George Bodenheimer, the president of ESPN and ABC's sport's division. Bodenheimer started in the mailroom, and through the years he was successful in attaining promotions. He now serves as the CEO of one of the top performing sports companies in the country. Bodenheimer continues to be successful because he knows the business from the bottom to the top. He has proven his worth leading on a smaller scale before he took on more reigns of responsibility. This same principle holds true for the presidency of the United States: a presidential candidate must prove his worth as a governor before vying for the job as the leader of the free world. This move will most certainly encourage great leaders to help their states first before trying to go straight to the White House. It will also reduce the expense and traditional mudslinging of a presidential election because we are dealing with fewer very qualified candidates. The only exception to the governor rule would be the Vice President. The vice president would not have to be a governor and potentially could become president when there may be an unfortunate early departure of the president.

Unlike business executives, however, political figures need to focus all of their energy on one position at a time. If political figures are too busy looking for their next position (i.e. getting re-elected as Senator or trying to go from governor of Ohio to President of the United States), their job performance suffers from their inattention. The tragic demise of Illinois's former governor, Rod Blagojevich, is a clear example of the potential for corruption, greed, and lack of focus when running for public office while in another political position.

On November 4, 2008, Barack Obama was elected President of the United States. By December 9, former Governor Blagojevich was arrested. He was charged with trying to sell President-Elect Obama's U.S. Senate seat. In part, I believe, he was inspired by Obama's move from state-level politics to the power and prestige granted to players in the federal realm. Basically, he was intoxicated by the possibility of making more money so he offered the seat in exchange for the position. If Obama weren't a senator during his bid to run for the presidency, Blagojevich wouldn't have been placed in such a position to sell the seat.

***

Possible mismanagement due to the distractions of

filling political vacancies left behind by incumbent presidents is not the only issue related to elections. The election system also has the potential to be huge vacuums that suck up money, time, and other valuable resources. The United States federal system is entering into one of the most important election cycles in history. Between now and the next election day, very little will be accomplished by the challengers who are running for election. Billions of dollars will be spent to vie for the presidency, while local communities suffer because their representatives are not doing their jobs. With the looming fiscal cliff that our country is facing, the United States could suffer financial chaos because the budget must be decided only one month after the election. Not to mention that every minute our National debt grows by $10,000,000. We need to stop this crime of overspending and over-owing.

We have allowed Senators and Congressmen to acquire too much power. I think that there is a crime here. After Franklin Delano Roosevelt, the President was only allowed to serve two terms of office. Congressmen and senators need this same restriction. The crime is that some federally elected leaders have violated the Sherman Anti-Trust Act by holding thirty-year monopolies on their seats. To make matters worse, career politicians have lost touch with knowing how things outside of politics work. You cannot limit terms in one branch of government as that changes the balance of power. Congress and Senate routinely take advantage of the "lame duck President" while not being subject to the same rules. Take the words of former Senator George McGovern, who tried unsuccessfully to build a career as a businessman after eighteen years in Congress: "I wish I had known a little more about the problems of the private sector.... I have to pay taxes, meet a payroll -- I wish I had a better sense of what it took to do that when I was in Washington." [iv] I believe McGovern is acknowledging the crime of the federal election system. Too much time in the system means not enough time and understanding of the needs of the American business and the people these businesses employ.

This ignorance of the inner workings of the private sector is a shameful example of the state of affairs in Congress. Congress should not be perched on Mt. Olympus. They should be on the ground with the same people who trust them with their livelihoods. The Hill shouldn't be a one-way trip to a full-time career as a federal politician. In order to be effective leaders, politicians need to have an understanding and connection to the commercial and business sectors of the United States. As Dan Greenberg wrote in his critique of Congressmen staying too long in their seats, "Ensuring that Members eventually are exposed to life outside of Congress should inculcate a more sophisticated understanding of the logic and the limits of federal regulation." [v] Greenberg is calling attention to the value of having a first-hand understanding of the effects of the laws that are passed through Congress. For example, Congressmen with experience in the business world will have a better understanding of how overregulation affects commerce in modern America. And these Congressmen will be able to come up with better laws that respond directly to the needs of the American people, especially if those representatives know that before too long they'll have to return to live in the world they've helped create. It's another way of forcing the people in charge of molding our world to have some skin in the game.

Between 1990 and 1994, twenty-three states limited service in their delegation to the United States Congress and Senate. In 1993, Arizona lawmakers enacted state legislation limiting the number of terms a politician could serve. This term limiting was short-lived. In *U.S. Term Limits v. Thornton*, the U.S. Supreme Court decided that state laws that set time-constraints on public office on the federal level were unconstitutional because states did not have the jurisdiction to enact legislation that went against long-held federal provisions of the Constitution. This decision was right; the Constitution does set the terms. So it's time to amend the Constitution.

***

Throughout this book, I will discuss many changes to the United States systems of governance. The first changes will be the five federal restructuring amendments that I discuss in this chapter: implementing the line-item veto power for the president; establishing new term limits for federal politicians; modifying requirements for running for political office; revamping federal districts to reflect geographical longitude and latitude lines; and changing compensation and benefits for elected officials. As King, I will use these seven royal amendments to restructure the United States federal election process and the Executive's power over legislation. These changes will bring the country to the twenty-first century. By modernizing U.S. governance, I will be doing what is best for all Americans and American Businesses.

My intention is not to make the United States into a permanent Kingdom. Make no mistake, I believe in the democratic systems that make up our country's government. However, I think these systems need to be evaluated and significantly repaired. Ultimately, bringing responsibility for governance back to the local and regional authorities is what's best for the United States. My seven royal amendments will begin the process of making the federal government smaller and hence, more efficient.

Line-Item Veto

Clinton was not given a sufficient amount of time to

realize the full genius of the line-item veto's effectiveness. Bush and Obama could have used this power to prevent delays passing budgets and other acts. This is a shameful missed opportunity for our country. I believe that the benefits of the line-item veto would have taken some time to be fully actualized. Bills combining different issues are ineffective and purposely misleading. Earmarks are a systemic problem, and the only way to stop them is with the line-item veto. This royal amendment will promote honest law-making because Congressmen will not be making laws through deception and partisanship rather through transparent and open methods. This deception in law-making assumes that the American people will never catch wise and, in so doing, displays contempt for the men and women who make up this nation. It should be a crime. Everything in the bill must be relevant to the topic of that bill. For example, bow and arrow research can't appear in a bill about highways.

While we are on the topic of lawmakers doing what's best for the U.S., bills will no longer be named after politicians. This egotistical practice is nothing more than a self-serving act showing no interest in what is best for the United States.

My line-item veto amendment will stop these practices and it will take the money out of the crime in several ways. In order to influence legislation, special interests will have to get the attention of the president and his officials. With the increased power of the line-item veto and no way to pass the buck to congress, the President will know that all eyes are on him. It will become very difficult to allow changes to slip by without Americans having a clear idea of who to hold accountable. Lobbyists will no longer be permitted to woo Congressmen to put their platforms into bills without each interaction becoming full public record. This legislation will minimize the insertion of unrelated facets into bills, leading to the curtailment of special interest groups vying for backroom favors from Congressmen and Senators. As a result, the bills submitted to the President by Congress will become succinct enough to address the issues. While this will increase the number of bills, earmarks will be eliminated and so will the potential for sneaking in extraneous topics and pork barrel, crony-beneficial funding which not only make otherwise excellent bills problematic, but which also bog down the political process. Recall that the excruciating slowness of our government is one of the reasons we need the broad, sweeping changes of a kingship in the first place in order to align our nation with the times. The more we erase the superfluous hurdles, the better our government will be at keeping up with the needs of citizens in the modern world.

The line-item veto will give the president a new elimination authority. He will not be able to add to the proposed bills, only deleting areas and sections that he thinks are unnecessary. The president is the Chief Executive Officer of our country. Because he is elected by all voting-age Americans, the President will be held responsible for allowing or disallowing certain bills and the content in those bills. He will be rewarded or punished in the next election and in history by what he leaves in or takes out of a bill. The line-item veto royal amendment will slow down if not outright eliminate the special interest groups and this will give Americans one person to blame if the bill does not succeed. After years of suffering from lack of accountability, this line-item veto will fill a desperate need to know who is making decisions in our government.

Qualifications

My new Qualifications Amendment will ensure that local communities do not suffer while politicians vie for a federal position. Allowing local and state politicians to continue making important state and local decisions related to energy efficiency, educational proficiency, and other key issues will ensure that the community runs without interruptions from federal freak shows like Congressional, Senate and Presidential elections.

The second royal amendment lays down three provisions: first, politicians may not run for a different office while holding another public office. In order to be elected into a different position the individuals must be "all-in." Running for any office is a full-time job, one that will distract and detract from the work needing attention on the local level. Incumbents are the only exception to this new provision, as they may be permitted two or three terms and these terms may be consecutive. This provision will allow the people who want to serve the country to show a commitment to serving as the leader of the free world. This privilege deserves dedication to the idea that local governments must be permitted to run business as usual for their communities.

The second provision runs in the same vein as not running for federal office while still serving in another office. Politicians and their executive staffs who leave office will have to wait out a two-year ethic period prior to seeking a job in a field related to their political or executive career. For example, Senator Debbie Stabenow of Michigan chairs the United States Committee on Agriculture, Nutrition, and Forestry. With this new provision, Senator Stabenow may not immediately obtain a job in any of these three sectors. She must wait two years before working as a lobbyist for a company like Monsanto or as a director of a food company. This levels the playing field and attempts to eliminate the possibility for corruption. Using a political position to fatten one's pockets at the expense of fair play for Americans is bad for the country. With the rules as they currently stand, every step she makes on the Senate's Committee on Agriculture, Nutrition, and Forestry can be potential for corruption.

However, with this new 2-year ethics period rule, we will take the money out of the crime. With no avenue to personal profit through political favors to entities that are not the American people the crime will go away.

The third provision of the Qualifications Amendment will require all presidential candidates to have served as a governor of a state. Throughout America's history, many of the great presidents served as governors before taking on the head position of the Executive Department. Thomas Jefferson, Theodore Roosevelt, Franklin Delano Roosevelt, Ronald Regan and Bill Clinton all served as governors of their states before rising to the federal level.[vi] These presidents passed the ultimate litmus test: they were able to run their states effectively enough to gain national attention. If a Presidential-hopeful can effectively run a state, with all its complexities and agencies, then he or she is ready to serve as president of all the states. As such, candidates will need to have served as governor at some point prior to entering a race to become the President of the United States.

These three provisions—holding no political office while running for another office, waiting for two years before working in a field similar to your political work and serving as governor before running for president—make up my second royal amendment. The Qualifications Amendment will enact political conditions allowing candidates to run for the presidency without detracting from and, by extension, preventing neglect of the local communities. Ultimately, this distraction-free election process will allow the federal and local politicians to focus on accomplishing what should be the inherent goal of all federal, state, and local political leaders around the country: doing what's best for the United States by doing what is best for the every state and community. Adjusting the qualifications for federal politicians will take the money out of the crime, and the crime will go away.

Restructuring Districts

The third royal amendment will ensure that all districts are fairly and equitably distributed along longitudinal and latitudinal lines. Gerrymandering will be eliminated; every United States citizen deserves the right to vote for his federal representative on a fair basis. Each state will determine the size of their box-shaped districts. And these boxes will be the same across the state and/or county. They will no longer look like Rorschach tests. This prohibition of gerrymandering will eliminate any manipulation or fixing of the election. Manipulation of elections will always be considered a treasonable offense.

Term Limits

Another federal restructuring amendment will focus on limiting the number and length of terms for federally elected officials. Congress, Senate and the Executive will be impacted by these new term limits.

Congress

The House of Representatives shall be composed of Members chosen every second Year by the People of the several States... [vii]
Article 1, Section 1, U.S. Constitution

When the Constitution was written, two years in office was a very long time for a Congressman and this length of time was sufficient to accomplish the goals of his candidacy. However, at that time, there were only thirteen states and, hence, far fewer interests that needed attention. Today, with fifty states and the varied viewpoints of 21st century multicultural America, two years has become an insufficient amount of time to accomplish much of anything. Almost as soon as Congressmen assume their positions in Washington, they must begin campaigning for their next term in office. It's not an effective use of time to have our Congressmen and women expending more of their energy on the campaign trail rather than instilling change for the good of the country within the halls of Congress. Americans need members of Congress to focus their energies on doing what's best for the country. They can do this by making decisions that keep our country modern.

I will eliminate the stagnation that happens during the Congressional election years. This two-year cycle effectively puts our country out of business every other year. No business can operate like that. As with every elected federal office, I will limit the number of times a federal politician may run for re-election. With this limit, people who come to Congress will truly represent the constituencies in their communities. Infusing new blood into the House will revitalize the commitment and the drive of its members to do what's best for the United States. With deadlines in place, Congressmen will have a stronger incentive to ensure all of the important programs pass and that they pass efficiently.

As King, I'd amend Article 1, Section 1 of the Constitution of the United States. The term of office in the House of Representatives will be extended from two to four years, and they may not serve longer than three terms. Congress just like the Senate will have alternating elections so all of congress will no longer be running for election or reelection at the same time. Again, this keeps the federal government in business and stops the biannual shutdown of the United States that happens as a result of the election. The length of each U.S. Senator's term will remain the same; however members of the U.S. Senate can now serve only two terms. Senators will represent one half of each state.

By changing the means for and the terms of becoming a Senator or Congressmen, those politicians who are elected will not waste time when they come to Washington. From day one of their service, they will begin doing what is best for the United States.

The Executive:
Making the Presidency Crime-free & Hip

The executive Power shall be vested in a President of the United States of America. He shall hold his Office during the Term of four Years ...[viii]
Article 2, Section 1, U.S. Constitution

No person shall be elected to the office of the President more than twice...[ix]
Amendment XXII, U.S. Constitution

I will amend Article 2, Section 1 of the Constitution by changing the presidential election process and requirements for this Presidential election process. The first section of the new amendment will address the length of time a President could hold office. Much like Congress, where two years is not long enough to get much accomplished, the President needs more time to bring his agenda to fruition. While I will not change the number of terms, I will extend the length of terms from four to six years. This extension means the longest period of time that any one president could hold office will now be twelve instead of eight years. With these term lengths, the President of the United States will be able to take the time he needs to accomplish his platforms and, by accomplishing his goals, the president will be focusing on what's best for the United States. Have you ever heard a president or presidential-hopeful articulate a four-year plan is? NO. It is always their five-year plan. Well, here you go, you now have six years, and I seriously doubt that we are going to hear or believe a candidate who is talking about a seven-year plan.

Next, the new amendment will make the election process more transparent and less for sale. The crime in the election cycle stems from the money contributions from people or organizations whose agendas may not sync up with what most benefits Americans on the whole. Yet, candidates need substantial sums of cash to run in a presidential race. Where will leaders get the money for their campaigns? Simple solution: they won't need it. The problem will be eliminated by taking the money out of the primary election cycle.

The first thing I will do is eliminate the outdated electoral college. Our presidents should be directly elected by their constituencies. I will never allow another Gore-Bush 2000 debacle to happen in our country again. Next, I will make pre-primaries similar to "America's Got Talent," a game show that allows Americans to showcase their skills for which the audience and remote viewers vote. Their votes are designated for participants that they think are the most talented. Like "America's Got Talent," every qualified candidate who would like to join the race may enter the competition. Instead of performing a song or dance, the candidates will showcase their qualifications through a series of debates and presentations that show their platform for the Presidency. Since we will be dealing with Governors and or former governors—unlike America's Got Talent—the competition will be highly informative and not a joke. The audience—American voters from around the world—will cast their ballots by calling in with their voter registration number. This whole process will happen on live television, which will encourage more voter involvement in the process from the beginning. Americans will see that they really can make a difference, understand the issues, and show them that their vote matters. This competition will be open to all parties and independents.

That means it will be extended beyond the typical Republican versus Democrat election process.

Let's be frank: Presidential elections are popularity contests. Ideally, a candidate's popularity would be determined on the merit of their ideas, not to how many people with whom they exchanged political favors for campaign dollars prior to assuming an office. This new process will even the playing field. Once each party has no more than four candidates, the candidates will level-up and the traditional primary will begin. In the past, presidential hopefuls have held onto senate and congressional seats, governorships, and other political offices while campaigning. As I said earlier, this will stop under my kingship. If you want to compete in the elections, you must not be holding any political office. Period. This will limit the number of candidates who are just running to create unnecessary turmoil for the strongest candidates and or hoping to make enough noise to be selected as a Vice President or Secretary of State.

The final provision of the new term-limit amendment will make tampering with elections a treasonable offense. Once my four-year reign as King has ended, the sanctity of presidential elections must be retained. In order to get rid of partisanship, and in order to focus our energy on doing what's best for America, the elected officials will not be committed to the party-line, rather to figuring out the best way to make American communities self-sufficient and economically prosperous.

By modifying the length and number of terms of U.S. Congressmen, Senators, and Presidents, the federal government will return to being an entity that needs to be run. Not an entity that needs to be run for.

Congressional Pay

They sell us the president the same way
They sell us our clothes and our cars
They sell us everything from youth to religion
The same time they sell us our wars
I want to know who the men in the shadows are
I want to hear somebody asking them why
They can be counted on to tell us who our enemies are
But they're never the ones to fight or to die .
Jackson Browne, Lives in the Balance.

My final federal restructuring amendment addresses the compensation and benefits for the President, Congressmen, and Senators. Congressional spending will have to feel the pain of American citizens; they can't have entitlements that aren't available to their constituents. As for healthcare, retirement, and other benefits, the President and members of Congress and Senate will receive the same package offered to the military. All former officials will feel the new changes as well. They were unethical when they gave themselves lifetime retirement packages. If there is one point upon which virtually every American can agree, it's that our government should be run ethically (at least, everybody who doesn't have an office on Capitol Hill). So I will be taking away the opulent retirement/benefits packages from previous representatives. If it's good enough for the military, it's good enough for Congress. Serving in Washington should be a privilege that citizens should embrace for the cause of improving the country instead of a promise of wealth regardless of how well an official performs.

In his 1961 inauguration speech, President Kennedy charged the country to, "Ask not what your country can do for you, but to ask what you can do for your country." Politicians need to apply this sense of altruism as they are serving the federal government of the United States. The privilege of holding the office must be the biggest benefit that motivates political leaders to serve their country. If our politicians are rewarded for being selfish, our government will be selfish to the consternation of the people it serves.

All current and previously elected officials will be held to this standard, and that will include a retroactive change of pay and benefits based on the new way of doing things. This retroactive pay standard will mean that some people will have to pay back the money disbursed; while others will be given more money.

Congressmen will be paid based on the average annual income of their constituents and the President will be paid based on the average annual income of everyone in the United States. Neither Congressmen nor Senators can be paid more than 3.5 times the median household income of their respective districts. The president will be paid no more than 6 times that figure. So based on 2006 figures, the national average annual income was $50,233. That means that the average Congressman or Senator will be paid around $150,699; and the highest a President can be paid is $301,398. The figure will be based on the median household income that existed the year they were elected into office.

Further, in order to get paid, Congressmen need to pass their budget. If they don't pass the budget, they and all other elected officials will simply not be paid. All those not being paid will also not be allowed to accrue any compensation until there is an approved budget. If money is the motivation, then they'll have to do the work to get paid.

It is clear that Congressmen are getting too comfortable in their "cushy" positions "up on the hill." Senators and Members of the House need to be among their constituents in order to understand how to represent them and show America that they have taken their hands out of the cookie jar. If they're unwilling to do so on their own, easy changes like this should be enough to force their hands out until we, their employers, say it's ok to have one.

***

My five federal restructuring amendments will lay the foundation for dramatic changes across all levels of the government. These changes will begin a shift from the centralized, big federal government to a de-centralized federal government that puts the strength of the people back into the hands of their community. Rather than telling members of local politicians how to run their local communities, the federal government will empower communities. In Part-Two, I will address how each executive department and some select agencies will be maintained, modified, or eradicated. To ensure that these changes that I put into effect are not undone after I leave office, I will put a law into effect that indicates all changes may not be altered for ten years after my Kingdom is over. After I leave my office as King, to pass any constitutional amendment must go back to the required 2/3rds vote.

Two: Taxes & National Debt Solved

The Congress shall have power to lay and collect taxes on incomes, from whatever source derived, without apportionment among the several states, and without regard to any census or enumeration.[x]

The Sixteenth Amendment of the U.S. Constitution

The Sixteenth Amendment is not working: fifty-one percent (51%) of Americans do not pay income tax.[xi] Without collection of an adequate amount of taxes, America suffers while the country is put further and further into debt. The good hardworking Americans are getting the shaft and paying for the majority. This is a crime that I will eliminate. If you work hard, you will be rewarded. As King, my royal cabinet and I will develop a method for maintaining a balanced budget and I will create an entirely different tax system.

The goal of this systemic restructuring will be two-fold:
1.) Create a system of taxes that will allow all people living in and visiting America to pay their fair share; and
2.) Make a focused plan to eliminate the national debt.

I will create a system of taxes based on consumption and based on this collection of taxes; I have generated a plan to be debt-free by the year 2045. Further, I have made a plan to have saved twenty-percent (20%) of the Gross Domestic Product (GDP) by the year 2070. First, I will turn my attention to the details of the consumption tax.

National Consumption Tax: A System for Modern America

If you were to go back and try to find and review the ratification of the 16th amendment...if you went back and examined that carefully, you would find that a sufficient number of states never ratified that amendment.

U.S. District Court Judge James C. Fox, 2003

The Sixteenth Amendment has led us to the current federal income tax system, with its many confusing loopholes and countless exemptions. Every year there are thousands of changes that even the best CPA can't keep up with or understand. This is an ineffective way to tax our citizens! This amendment is unfair, ineffective, and inefficient.

Under my rule, we will eliminate all federal taxes except one. That means eliminating all personal and corporate income tax and all of the special loop-holes and implement a national consumption tax. Capitalism predominates as the economic system in the United States. The tax that will be the most effective in our country will target a consumer society's system of spending and buying products that are in the marketplace. Taxing the consumption rather than the income of Americans will fix the loopholes so that everyone from those who don't work (stay at home moms, disabled, destitute) up through billionaires who have grown accustomed to avoidance of paying income and sales tax.

A twelve percent (12%) consumption tax on non-essential goods will replace all federal income taxes, including individual and corporate income taxes. Special additional consumption taxes will be instated for certain products like alcohol, tobacco, gasoline, marijuana etc. Under the National Consumption Tax Amendment, all life necessities will be exempt from taxation. Because these items are required by everyone to survive, no American will pay taxes for water, food, and other compulsory survival items. The privilege of eating food that you've purchased should not be something for which you must additionally pay Uncle Sam. Conversely, all luxury and non-essential goods will be subject to taxation at the time of purchase. Boats, cosmetic plastic surgery, and other optional items fall into these luxury and non-essential goods category. Chart 1 shows some examples of goods that will and will not be taxed.

Americans spent over 60 trillion dollars on consumer products in 2011.[xii] If we were taxing half of those expenditures at a rate of twelve percent (12%), the federal government would be able to collect two trillion dollars a year in taxes without paying tax collectors billions of dollars to do so. With the consumption tax, we'll be regaining the millions of dollars of uncollected revenue that we are currently losing from the underground economy. This underground economy comes from people who are working such as undocumented illegal immigrants and migrants. However, this economy should also include people who visit the country and people who are participating in illegal activities.

Now they'll have to pay taxes every time they buy luxury items, including items that are purchased over the internet. The moratorium on taxing internet transactions will be completely over. This will also access those who are not employed because they are unable to for reasons of being underage, disabled, a housewife or husband, and retired. If they are buying luxury goods, then they can afford to pay a twelve percent (12%) tax on these non-essential purchases. There is a whole underground economy. We need to include the fifty-one percent (51%) of Americans who are not paying their fair share. With a national consumption tax, everyone will pay their share and America will benefit from implementing such a fair system of taxation.

One downside of my system will be the annihilation of the accounting industry. However, the growth of other industries due to the consumption tax will make up for the decimation of the accounting industry. Captain Picard from Star Trek once said, "The good of the many outweigh the good of the few." The benefits from the new consumption tax far outweigh the negatives because the tax will be fair, broad based and it will be for everyone. More importantly everyone will understand it. Further, this downside will be counterbalanced by the return of industry. Because of this new consumer and corporate friendly system of taxes, companies that have left the United States will return. Multinational companies will return hundreds of billions of dollars to the United States that have been stuck offshore because of our existing tax structure.

Necessities (untaxed)	Luxury Items (taxed)
Water & Non-prepared food	Boat
Required OTC & Prescribed procedures & medications	Airplane
Toilet paper, feminine products, diapers	Car
non-luxury clothes	Jewelry
Required school supplies	home improvements
	beauty treatments
	Alcohol
	elective health care frozen foods

Chart 1: Examples of Necessity v. Luxury Items.

Personal tax havens will no longer be necessary. That newfound money will be spent in the US leading to the rebuilding or upgrading of manufacturing facilities, which will allow more Americans to work.

As the consumption tax replaces the federal taxation system, this new system will not intervene with how states tax their citizens. Although states will still be permitted to tax as they see fit, this new federal consumption tax will force them to re-think their current structures. Boat levies exemplify how states will need to adjust their tax systems to compete with other states. For example, people from Rhode Island do not pay property tax on boats but people in South Carolina do. In order to remain viable contenders in the free market, South Carolina will need to rethink its system or lose citizens and their revenue.

Because we are in a recession, this is the ideal time to switch over to a consumption-based tax structure. If we were in the middle of a boom, this new tax system will likely temporarily affect the economy in a negative way because people will be spending less money. But because people are already spending and making less money, America is at an ideal time to transition to this new system of taxation.

Getting rid of income tax includes getting rid of corporate, dividend, and interest income tax. Simply put, any income—even if its corporate income—is not taxable. Americans will be expected to reinvest or spend it. Either option is good for the US, as it will enliven the pool of money that goes back into the economy.

Corporate Taxation & Payment to the Government

This new system would simplify taxes for businesses, so that the companies upgrade their assets, which creates jobs so that companies can hire more people. They will save money because they will no longer have to file quarterly tax returns and social security tax and other entitlements will be eliminated (*see Chapter Four*). This change will allow business owners to spend money on their product and their people.

American corporations will be taxed in the same way that individuals are taxed. For example, the transcriptionist is paid a full wage, while the person who buys the transcript will pay a twelve percent (12%) tax that will in-turn be submitted to the government by the company that supplies the transcript. Another example comes from restaurants. If you sit down and eat at a restaurant, you will pay a consumption tax on the food and beverages that you purchase. If you go to a grocery store and buy flour, cheese, pepperoni you won't pay any tax but if you buy a premade frozen pizza you pay the tax. The ultimate side effect will be healthier eating (which, itself, will lower the cost of medical coverage). Finally, school supplies will be exempt when they are purchased through the school. This will create a brand new industry. As an example, Staples may create a partnership with a school and sell items that are tax exempt, making money for the school system.

Implementing the national consumption tax adds no additional burden for recordkeeping of small or big business and it significantly reduces the costs of both local and federal governments. In 45 of the 50 states, there is already a sales tax. That means only Alaska, Delaware, Montana, New Hampshire, and Oregon will need to adjust or have federal consumption tax adjusters implementing a system for them. For most businesses in the US, we're going to streamline the process for all consumption income tax collection. Whether a multinational corporation or a small-town mom-and-pop shop, a universal form will be available for all businesses across the country. So it will not matter if a business sold something in Virginia or California. Whatever you owe will be submitted to the IRS on a monthly basis. Monitoring of tax collection will be a whole lot easier because the 45 states that are already collecting sales tax have a collection system in place.

This system of tax collection will be far easier. Businesses will not have an added burden—they already collect this kind of information. Since businesses are already accustomed to collecting and paying state sales tax. The federal government will tap into the already existing systems of tax collection. Every month, businesses can enter the number and have the appropriate amount automatically drafted out of their account into a state and federal tax fund. States that are not currently charging a sales tax will have a federal representative that audits the businesses in the state. This will likely push those five states without sales taxes to install their own systems, to ensure the local governments know what is going on with their businesses. Americans from 45 states will not have to worry about adding a layer of bureaucracy to collect this money. For example, Virginia currently has a five percent (5%) sales tax that they have to pay to the state. Instead of collecting only for the state, business will now collect seventeen percent (17%) tax to pay out to the State of Virginia and the federal government. For those of us paying current income tax 17% is a huge savings. For the 51% people paying nothing: too bad.

The Internal Revenue Service will work in a coordinated effort with states that are already charging sales tax to reduce or eliminate any additional burden to the businesses that are paying their taxes. These changes mean that the IRS budget and employees can probably be cut in half. Right now, the IRS has to literally manage and deal with 140.5 million tax returns a year. By going to a national consumption tax, we will have reduced it to less than 7 million because now the federal government will only be dealing with individuals and corporations who are selling products instead of every single person and company in America. Further, to police taxation has become easier, because the number of things you have to look at is significantly reduced. Every business owner will be required to file a return by the tenth of every month. If a business $100,000 of sales in November, then the business owes the government $12,000 by the tenth of December.

The loop-hole there, everybody's going to start buying stuff in a company, and instead of selling a house, I'm just going to sell you my company. This is called a change of control transaction. To eliminate this potential loop-hole there will be a national consumption tax charged in these cases. The charge will be based on the purchase price and or the book value whichever is greater. This is for any change of control transaction public or private. A change of control is determined by the Security and Exchange Commission. There are already formulas and already language on what the definition of change of control is, and that will eliminate the loophole.

Home-Owner and Industrial Relief Tax	
2013	2.5%
2014	5%
2015	7.5%
2016	10%
2017	12%

Chart 2: Home-Owner and Industrial Relief Tax Plan.

This consumption system will have one temporary exception. Because of the current housing crisis, we will have some relief for homeowners and construction of industrial businesses. The consumption tax will be scaled down for home and industrial wares. This would include building materials, appliances, and furniture. This scale will increase over the course of four years giving Americans relief during these hard economic times, but anticipating that we'll be getting out this economic crisis as soon as possible. The scale will start at two and a half percent (2.5%) and it will increase over the next four years until it reaches twelve percent (12%). This relief plan will be applied to already existing primary residential homes and new industrial construction and modernization.

A Balanced Budget Amendment That Works

...100 percent (100%) of what is collected is absorbed solely by interest on the federal debt and by federal government contributions to transfer payments. In other words, all individual income tax revenues are gone

before one nickel is spent on the services that taxpayers expect from their government.

The Grace Commission, 1983

My plan to pay the national debt is appropriately called the Balanced Budget Amendment. The revenue generated from the new national consumption tax will be used to balance the budget, to attain a goal of financial equilibrium. An America in the state of Financial Equilibrium will be debt-free and will have savings equal to twenty percent (20%) of the GDP in an Emergency Relief Fund. This amendment will disallow the federal government from spending any more than ninety-percent (90%) of the Consumption tax raised in a given year. A mandatory minimum twelve percent (12%) of the taxes collected will be allocated to pay down the principle balance of the debt until we can begin saving. Barring any disaster or huge fluctuation in consumption tax revenue, Americans should be able to pay off the national debt no later than 2045 (see Chart 4). As such, by 2045, the U.S. will begin saving money rather than spending all the country's revenue to pay down interest alone.

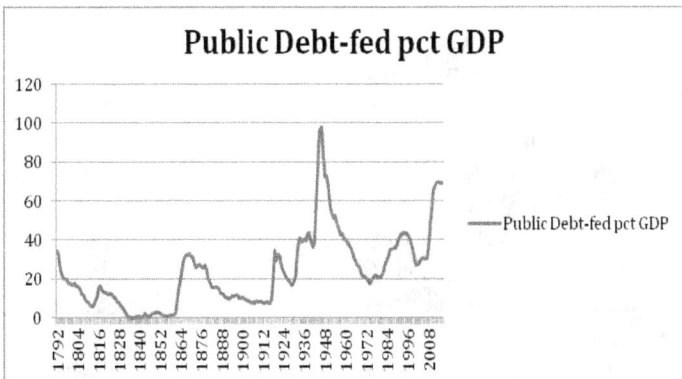

Chart 3: Federal Debt: Percentage of the GDP.[xiii]

This 90-10 formula will be in place until we are debt free and we have saved an Emergency Relief Fund that equals twenty percent (20%) of the GDP. The emergency funds can only be used for national emergencies declared by the president such as damage related to floods, earthquakes, hurricanes, and more. When the country's deficit is brought down to zero debt, we will continue to spend up to ninety percent (90%) of the consumption tax and a minimum of ten percent (10%) will go to saving for emergency funds until that savings reaches its ultimate goal: twenty percent (20%) of the GDP. Once the Emergency Relief Fund reaches twenty percent (20%) of the GDP, the consumption tax will be reduced from twelve percent (12%) down to ten (10%). Again, as long as our financial situation remains about the same, the federal government should have reached the Emergency Relief Fund goal no later than 2070. At that time, five percent (5%) of the consumption tax collected will be used to ensure we remain debt-free and to ensure that the emergency relief fund stays at twenty percent (20%) of the GDP. This tax will only be increased if we end a year in debt or the emergency relief fund falls below twenty percent (20%) of the GDP. Once debt and savings are returned to their state of equilibrium, the consumption tax will be returned to ten percent (10%).

In Chart 4, I have created a chart based on my calculations for paying down the national debt. As of July 2012, the national debt was approximately 15.9 trillion dollars.[xiv] This does not include the 60 trillion dollars in obligations that we have which is addressed later in the book. With my new consumption tax, I will be collecting twelve percent (12%) of the gross domestic product (GDP). In 2011, the GDP was 60.3 trillion dollars. Personal consumption expenditures were 42.9 trillion dollars. Personal consumption expenditures include goods and services. To factor in what my consumption tax will be collecting, I have used the figures from the GDP's personal consumption expenditures. The twelve percent (12%) consumption tax based on the 42.9 trillion dollars will be $5.149 trillion dollars. Since ten percent (10%) of the consumption tax collected will go towards paying down the national debt, $514.99 billion dollars will be used to pay the debt every year.

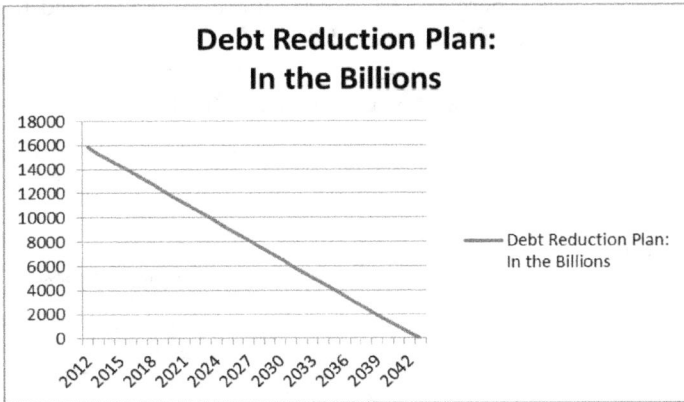

Chart 4: Debt Reducation Plan.

At that rate the national debt will be paid off no later than 2045. By 2070 the United States will have saved twenty percent (20%) of the GDP, or $12.060 trillion, by the year 2070.

Chart 5 shows my plan for accruing an Emergency Savings Plan that is twenty percent (20%) of the GDP. Starting in 2045, the federal government will continue to collect a twelve percent (12%) consumption tax based on the personal consumption expenditures and the government will continue to reserve ten percent (10%) of that consumption tax for the Emergency Savings Plan. Using the numbers above, again assuming that there are no huge fluctuations in the current $60.3 trillion dollar GDP, the government will be able to save $5.149 trillion dollars a year. As such, the United States will have saved twenty percent (20%) of the GDP, or $12.060 trillion, by the year 2070. At that time, the consumption tax may be reduced to ten percent (10%). The national consumption tax will remain at ten percent (10%) unless the Emergency Savings Plan goes below twenty percent (20%), at which time the government will be allowed to increase the consumption tax back to twelve percent (12%) until the fund is returned to twenty percent (20%) of the GDP.

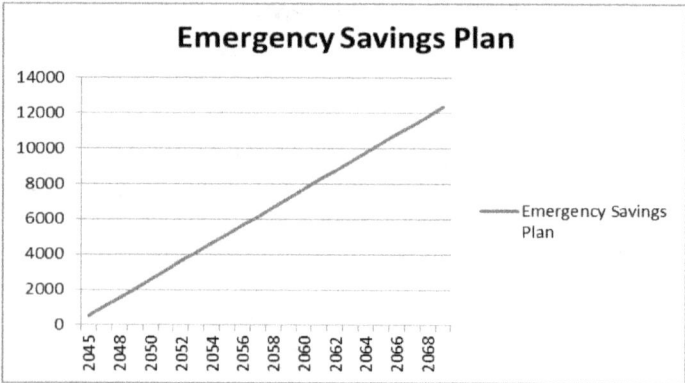

Chart 5: Emergency Savings Plan.

Once Congress has put together a budget that falls into this balanced budget amendment and with the new line-item veto, the President can eliminate lines he contends with rather than returning the entire budget to Congress. A more efficiently passed balanced budget amendment will allow officials to move forward and keep the government running efficiently and effectively without delays caused by unnecessary banter and political maneuvering. By eliminating the debt with this amendment, the United States will become a stronger, more independent nation without the constraints of and pressures from foreign interests. By eliminating these constraints, we will be doing what is best for America.

***

As you have seen, the royal amendments fall into two categories: budgetary and government restructuring. These changes will set the stage for considerable modification of the United States federal government. The next part of this book focuses on how I will change the currently existing departments of the Executive Branch.

PART TWO:

King's Departments

Revamped

Appointed Royal Cabinet Members by Department

Energy: **T. Boone Pickens, 64**

Treasury: **Arthur C. Brooks, 78**

Defense: **Lynn Tilton, 117**

Justice: **Brigadier General Judge James Cullen**

State: **Brent Scowcroft, 126**

Labor: **Jack Welch, 152**

Homeland Security: **Peter Thiel, 169**

Community Development & Sustainability:

Malone Mitchell III, 192

Consolidation, Coordination, & Ethics:

Rep David Camp, 217

Chart 6: Appointed Royal Cabinet Members

Introduction

I feel it only fair to warn readers now that things are about to start getting very technical. This is the foundation upon which the whole house is built, and scaffolding, though necessary, is never as appealing as the finished product. Bear with me, because the ideas are worth it.

Part Two of this book, contains an analysis of existing Executive Departments: Energy, Treasury, Defense, Justice, State, Labor, and Homeland Security. Each chapter begins with a status page that includes the following information about the department that will be the focus of the chapter: current and new mission statements, agencies and departments that have been consolidated into the new department, royal cabinet members chosen to lead the department, budget, and brief histories. I have reviewed each mission statement of the Departments of Energy, Treasury, Defense, Justice, State, Labor, and Homeland Security. During this review, I folded up agencies and--in some cases--departments that I believe will be more efficiently run within one of Part Two's Executive Departments. The agencies swallowed up by the remaining departments are listed on the second part of the status page. The third section of each department's status page names a royal cabinet secretary and, in some cases, their assistant secretaries. In Chart Six, I have listed my cabinet members by department. These are the people who will be very important for me to accomplish the goals for my Kingdom.

Obviously, one of the primary goals of consolidating and eliminating departments is to make the government run more efficiently in order to realize the goal of balancing the budget. One part to the plan is to start focusing on a custom that needs to stop in the federal government. Currently, agencies are given a certain amount of money at the beginning of the fiscal year. If they don't use all of their money, they are supposed to give that money back to the government. As such, employees of federal agencies and federal contractors scramble to use up all of their funding prior to the end of the fiscal year. Another thing they do is to spend it too fast and run out of money. They fall behind and hold projects off until October. Employees are even told not to submit expense reports until the next fiscal year. The agencies and contractors practice this use it or lose it policy for several reasons. Namely, they don't want to lose funding for the following calendar year. For example, the Department of Energy has a $29.5 billion dollar budget for the year 2012. If they have only spent 29 billion dollars by the end of August, the officials in that department will scramble to spend the remaining 500 million dollars, without consideration for whether or not that half a billion dollars needed to be spent. If they don't spend the $29.5 billion by September 30, 2012, they might be at risk for a budget cut for the 2013 fiscal year. This practice of use it or lose it is wasteful and counterproductive.

The federal government should incentivize agencies to go in under budget. Rather than punish the agency for going under budget, I will give them the same budget the next year. They will be rewarded with an extra cushion when they have earned it, not when they have misappropriated funds. This new incentive of keeping the same budget for the previous year if people go in at or under budget will kill use it or lose it and rewarding different agencies for going in under budget will also further promote that these agencies also submit accurate budgets.

My concern for this budgetary system is apparent in the fourth part of each chapter's information page. After listing the cabinet members, I show the budget for the 2010 and 2012 fiscal years. I obtained these figures from the report generated by the Executive Office of the President of the United States Fiscal Year 2012 Budget of the U.S. Government.[xv] I would have developed the fourth section of the details page by figuring out more fiscally responsible budgets for each of the departments. Finally, I include some key historical information in the fifth section of the status page. That information includes date established, law establishing the agency, and the historical need that led to the founding of the agencies.

As the King of the United States, I will find more and more ways to incorporate changes in order to cultivate free enterprise. My team of cabinet members and I will guide America to a better more fiscally responsible place. As the King of the United States, I will do what's best for the country by deregulating, eliminating wasteful spending, and consolidating programs.

Three: Energy

I.   Mission Statement

   A.)   2011: The mission of the Energy Department is to ensure America's security and prosperity by addressing its energy, environmental and nuclear challenges through transformative science and technology solutions.

   B.)   NEW: The mission of the Energy Department is to make the US secure and prosperous with the mandate of one hundred percent (100%) energy independence by 2016. This initiative will be accomplished by utilizing current resources and developing new technologies and sustainable methods through coordinated efforts with communities and governmental agencies.

II.   Agencies

   A.)   Nuclear Regulatory Commission

B.) Tennessee Valley Authority

III. Royal Secretary: T. Boone Pickens

IV. Budget:
Department of Energy Budget
1.) 2010: 12% less than 2012 budget
2.) 2012: 29.5 billion

V. History
A.) Established by the Department of Energy Organization Act of 1977 (P.L. 95-91, 91 Stat. 565)
1.) Consolidated various energy departments after the oil crisis of 1973.
2.) Law signed on August 4, 1977, went into effect on October 1, 1977

Introduction: New Energy Plans

All that foreign oil controlling American soil,
Look around you, it's just bound to make you embarrassed.
Sheiks walkin around like kings, wearing fancy jewels and nose rings,
Deciding America's future from Amsterdam and to Paris.
Bob Dylan, Slow Train

In "Dilithium Crystals "Most Likely" to Power Next Generation," Christine Patton of the Association for the Study of Peak Oil and Gas USA (ASPO-USA) stated that eighty-four percent (84%) of Americans have voted that dilithium crystals are the "most likely" fuel to power the cars of the future.[xvi] So what was once mere science fiction is becoming reality. Finding a practical use of the fuel that ran Star Trek's Starship Enterprise outranked other fuels such as corn ethanol, hydrogen, nuclear, shale gas and photovoltaic solar panels. And lest you think my giddiness for dilithium crystals in entirely due to my nerdery (instead of only partially), in that same article, Professor Stephen Palmer of MIT claims that the crystals have an "infinite capacity for power generation." He goes on to explain that the crystals provide enough power for starship warp drives, and if we could harness this energy source we'd be set for thousands of years.

Within the scientific community, a debate brews over the relevance of dilithium crystals on helping our energy crisis. Many government officials and environmentalists scoff at the idea of using dilithium crystals, calling it an "unproven technology." Raven Baker, spokesperson for a grassroots sustainability group called Transition US, refutes the claim that a fictional fuel is the key to the future. He claims that Americans should be proactive and not wait around for the government to create a miracle energy source. Instead, local communities should be working on conservation, growing food locally and organizing their towns and cities in a way that promotes the least amount of vehicular travel. On the other hand, some politicians believe we should increase funding for NASA to find space crystals like dilithium to harness energy. After all, according to the popular television series, "it is the fuel of tomorrow." I see no impediment to doing both. I contend that the energy fortitude of the United States will come from a combination of innovators with new viewpoints—a combination of dream big to discover more and dream local to continue current development.

America is our Starship Enterprise, and the more ways we find to produce effective fuel for her, the farther we can go." Under my government's energy plan, dilithium crystals, nuclear power, oil, and other fuel will factor into my modified Pickens' Plan that will try to attain the goal of energy independence for the United States. Such issues have deeper roots in previous eras of American history. One such period occurred in October 1973; the Egyptian and Syrian governments attacked Israel during Yom Kippur. When Nixon began sending remissions to help the young country of Israel, the Organization of Arab Petroleum Exporting Countries (OPEC) implemented an oil embargo against the United States.[xvii] OPEC's embargo was very effective in making Americans more than just uncomfortable and inconvenienced: the country was parallelized. Gas prices skyrocketed and gas was rationed. People didn't travel, and intrastate commerce came to a grinding halt. The five policies and eight departments involved with the energy in the United States were ineffective in addressing the problems that escalated as a result of the oil embargo.

Many Americans remember the long lines to get gas, but the impact was more far-reaching. According to a report written by Dylan Lee Lehrke about the Energy Crisis of the 1970s, "nonintegrated policy, jurisdictional confusion, poor economic advising, lack of coordination between states and the federal government, bureaucratic indifference, and sheer number of actors" led to stagnation and poor management of the crisis.[xviii] In short, too many cooks, too many ideas, and the soup was overdone. In the late 1970s, after the discordant Nixon era had already come to a close, two more pieces of legislation were passed: the Energy Policy & Conservation Act of 1975 and the Department of Energy Organization Act of 1977. Formed by the latter of these acts, the Department of Energy was formed to centralize the various existing agencies and organizations that were addressing energy issues.

Perhaps this department might have made more progress in establishing a more sustainable energy plan had oil prices not dropped in the 1980s. Alas, when oil and gas became accessible again, the Energy Department just became another government entity awash in the noise and ineffectiveness of Washington DC's beltway politics. This short-term memory post crisis was not always the way in

America. During World War II, Americans worked together in one of the most collaborative manners ever seen in the history of the United States. The common cause was the creation of supplies and wares that were necessary to win the war. People lived on food and energy rations, and while there may have been some hardships, Americans collaborated in a way that made sense for the greater good of the country. Our peoples came together to produce the technology and energy needed to defeat the Axis powers in Europe and the Pacific. During this time, many projects were instituted that promoted a greater sense of duty and responsibility to the community of the United States.

One such project that exemplifies when Americans did what's best for the country occurred during World War II with the Manhattan Project. This coordinated effort lead to the development of a new form of energy: Nuclear Power. Nuclear power was necessary for the development of new power plants, fuel cells for ships, submarines, and planes. Formerly, the application of nuclear power led to the use of the atomic bomb, which has been argued to be a requirement for the end of the war on the Pacific front.

The City of Oak Ridge, Tennessee grew up around this secret military project. Families were relocated to what was then a rural part of the state. Only a few knew precisely why they were in Oak Ridge, but they knew they were developing a new form of energy that would allow the U.S. to compete on the world stage in unprecedented ways. The men and women dedicated to this mission committed many hours and days to a successful project for the good of the country. The Department of Defense transplanted Americans to the city of Oak Ridge Tennessee to harness a new form of energy: nuclear power.

In order to solve our current dependence on foreign energy sources, Americans need the same level of focus and commitment that they had in the Forties. The leaders and people will have to be myopic in their drive to ensure that the problems related to establishing energy independence are solved. In 2008, T. Boone Pickens unveiled his multifaceted plan for improving energy production in America. The Pickens Plan pushes against oil addiction and promotes a more self-sufficient United States.

The key elements of the Pickens Plan will ensure energy independence and energy efficiency through incentives for individuals and corporations to use diversified energy, and development of an enhanced power-grid capability. I take this one step further by allowing local leaders to figure out what is most sustainable for their communities. Through a collaborative effort with federal representatives, the Energy Department will serve as a coordinator rather than a top-down adjudicator of these locally-driven plans. The federal government will do what it's hired to do: doing what's best for the American people by guiding communities to become self-sufficient energy producers. Let the people of North Carolina find out what works best for them, and do not impose those standards on Texans. At the same time, politicians need to work nationwide to diversify energy production and reach the goal of one hundred percent (100%) self-sustainability.

We need to stop giving money to people who hate our way of life. The United States needs to stop purchasing energy resources from countries with the most terrorists. If we are able to harness the "dilithium crystal" or any other new, sustainable power source that replaces our dependence on oil, what would happen to the power of the Middle East? What better way to win the "War on Terror" than to stop funding nations that house these terrorists. By working with our allies to eliminate reliance on foreign sources of energy and by empowering communities to come up with their own energy solutions, America and the world will become more powerful.

The crime in energy relates to the lack of coordination and the lip-service given by the Department of Energy to use "transformative science and technology solutions." As I have done with each executive department's mission statement, the Department of Energy will be bringing the problems of energy back to the community. As I see it, the crimes at the Department of Energy relate to funneling resources to develop the wrong type of energy. The Pickens Plan will be the best route to implementing and maintaining a sustainable, multi-faceted approach that will allow the U.S. to obtain energy independence.

Energy Task Force

We've got all these politicians talking about better health care and what all, but believe me, we're not going to have the money to take care of sick people—or anyone else as far as I'm concerned—if we don't fix our energy problem right now. I've got an idea what to do. [xix]

T. Boone Pickens

Energy independence will be the first priority of my term as King of the United States. I will appoint Mr. T. Boone Pickens to work as the head energy representative on my royal cabinet. Pickens is one of the leading energy magnates in America. Born in 1928 in Oklahoma, his father was an oil and mineral landsman. After graduating from college, he used his degree in geology to work at Phillips Petroleum. This work led him to establish Mesa Petroleum, which by 1981 grew into one of the largest independent oil companies in the world. Pickens was able to develop Mesa by acquiring a series of other companies. He established BP Capital Management in 1997, an investment company focused on energy development. In 2009, he received the Bower Award for Business Leadership for his leadership in energy production (oil, domestic renewable energy, etc.) and his philanthropy with education, medical research, and wildlife conservation. He established Clean Energy Fuels Corp in 1997, an energy corporation with a focus on

PART TWO

promoting natural gas as the best substitute for oil because it is homegrown.

By 2008, he had enough experience in the energy sector to develop the Pickens Plan. His proposal for the greater use of natural gas in heavy duty trucks and fleet vehicles is included in NAT GAS Act (H.R. 1835 and S. 1408) and the American Power Act. The American Power Act, drafted by Joseph Lieberman and John Kerry, promotes a change to environment, national security, and economy that they hope would lead to energy efficiency through a coordinated effort between different sectors of American Society. The coordination will come from the defense, religious, and political sectors who will limit foreign dependence on oil by promoting the use of diversified energy sources. Further, this plan's aim is to reduce the environmental impact of energy emissions. Finally, the American Power Act proposals will create a number of jobs as these new systems and their infrastructures are developed. I will discuss both of these acts in more detail in Defense and Homeland Security Chapters.

As my Department of Energy royal cabinet expert, Pickens will address the issues relevant to ensuring United States self-sufficiency: energy systems and their management, the development of relevant science and technology, and energy safety and security. One goal of the Pickens Plan is to have seventy-five percent (75%) of America's energy come from domestic sources. I will charge Pickens and other leaders in the energy sector to come up with and implement a plan that will make the United States one hundred percent (100%) energy independent over the next four years. We made it to the moon didn't we? Getting energy independent should be a piece of cake then.

With current population levels, this energy independence is imperative for America's economic comeback. Until the turn of the Twentieth Century, the world population remained constant. The discovery of oil prompted unprecedented population growth leading to a huge spike that you see in the chart below. Up until the late 19th century, the population remained less than a billion people worldwide. In 1900, that number doubled, though remained less than two billion people. By 2000, there were six billion people living in the world. This phenomenal population growth will no longer be sustainable unless we come up with alternative means for producing efficient and effective energy sources that will work for our country. Today, the United States obtains over sixty-five percent (65%) of its oil from foreign sources. Under my new Energy Department's plan, the country would strive to eliminate all use oil supplied by other countries.

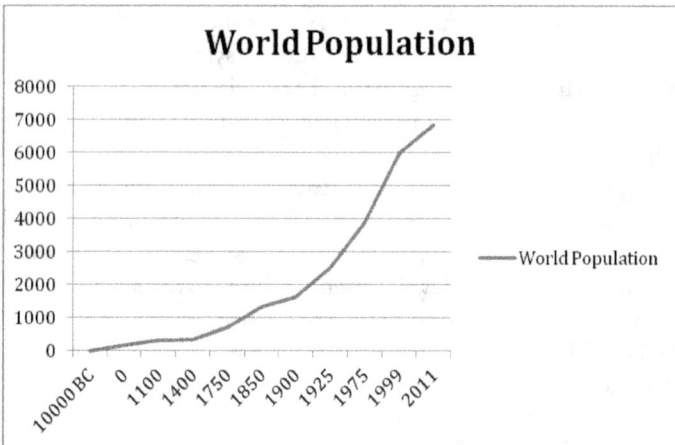

Chart 7: World Population, Then and Now.[xx]

Resources are finite, so the best plan will include multiple methods of obtaining energy. When energy is no longer cheap, we need to localize how we obtain our goods and products. Fuel will be too expensive to continue shipping products to certain parts of the country. For example, importing certain foods to American communities will no longer be feasible. To continue to provide sufficient nourishment to regions around the country, these regions will have to be sustained by home-grown farms. As such, the Department of Agriculture will need to develop local community farming plans to avoid devastation once America makes the inevitable shift to more local energy resources.

The main goal of the Department of Energy will be to ensure that the US is one hundred percent (100%) energy independent in an environmentally friendly and self-sustainable manner by 2016. The people who will be hired to ensure that this project is completed will leave their egos and politics behind, and they will not stop working until the goal is achieved. The best scientists in the country will apply their skills to ensuring the implementation of the Pickens Plan. To first achieve this goal of energy sustainability, those with the skill and know-how to implement this plan will work like the heroes of Oak Ridge. Like the people committed to winning World War II, the experts will have the same heroism when they leave their egos behind to ensure energy independence.

Initially, the primary source of energy that the United States will promote will be natural gas. All oil and other energy sources will be subject to a consumption tax the way that all consumer goods purchased in this country are taxed. However, because we are encouraging a focus on natural gas, natural gas will only be subject to a five percent (5%) consumption tax for the next 5 years to encourage automobile and trucking companies to convert their fleets to natural gas.

On the other hand, Americans need to be disincentivized from consuming energy that is not effective or efficient to maintain. For example, all food-stock based ethanol will be abolished. That means no federal funds will go to corn based ethanol production. While ethanol has been argued to be more cost-effective than oil or gas, this cost-effectiveness only appears in the use of the fuel. Unfortunately, the energy used in the creation of this fuel is less cost-effective than oil or natural gas. Some might argue that it is a net negative energy. This argument comes from the fact that it takes more energy to make corn-based ethanol than the energy that it makes because of the fuel, delivery, and other associated costs that are required to distill this energy. As such, unless someone invents a more cost-effective way to produce ethanol, this form of energy is counter-productive. Corn based ethanol is simply not going to work and will be stopped. In a similar vein, the federal government will incentivize car manufacturers to improve fuel efficiency. If Americans want to drive a car that is not fuel efficient, they will be penalized with an increased consumption tax. Should any American want to continue using gas guzzlers, they will be penalized with an additional five percent (5%) energy tax on top of the already exist twelve percent (12%) consumption tax. That means if someone wants to buy a Land Rover for 50,000 dollars, the total tax for that land rover would be $8500. If someone wants to buy a "green" car, their consumption tax will be 5% less. For example, a person buying a Camaro will pay twelve percent (12%), while a person buying a Chevy Volt will pay seven percent (7%) consumption tax.

Because of the urgency of finding replaceable, renewable sources, all energy-related patents will have different rules than other patents. The Department of Energy will work with private enterprise to ensure full development of all feasible patents that could lead to establishing a more sustainable energy plan. Since the government is investing in these technologies, it will own its share or all of the patents and collect revenue that a typical investor would get. Right now the government loses rights to the patent that they put funding behind. Scientists end up getting rich off of government investment. This is a sweetheart deal for the scientists, who not only were given money to work on the idea but who also reap the financial rewards of instilling a successful invention into the consumer market. I will change this practice because it is not benefiting the U.S. I will make it so that the government receives the same market return on patent investments as the investors from private corporations. The sweetheart deals end here. Scientists with successful inventions will still make a lot of money but so will the government as his investor. Federal ownership of any patents that were created with federal funding is good for many reasons: first, federal funding for energy will be allocated to the companies that further develop clean, sufficient energy; and second, by making these patents accessible through public domain and or the federal government getting a return on the investment, the marketplace of ideas will have fewer restrictions placed on them. So, by allowing energy patents to be public domain, American companies and businesses will be incentivized to and not blocked from supporting the development of alternative forms of energy.

Another reason to loosen the hold on energy patents is to relinquish the Organization of Arab Petroleum Exporting Countries monopoly on available energy resources. As Americans, it is in our best interest to decrease our allies and America's reliance on energy that comes from OPEC sources and increase our use of American-generated energy sources. This self-reliance will eliminate several roadblocks to obtaining affordable, sustainable American energy. Right now, the cost of oil is determined by many factors in the market. However, the cost of getting oil out of the ground and to market does not change greatly. So when there are natural and man-made disasters like oil spills, hurricanes, and earthquakes, the oil prices go up and the company makes more money because of projected costs related to transportation and other losses. This crime of price adjustment will be eradicated if local energy sources are used because the demand and control of the oil will reside in the hands of our government, not other governments unsympathetic to our people.

Oil refineries are not being built in the U.S. these days. The last refinery that was constructed in the US is over thirty years old. By the admission of the oil company's CEO the demand for refineries has decreased because obtaining energy in this process is also declining. Yet, energy consumption is projected to increase fifty percent (50%) by 2030. With refineries decreasing in their output of oil, it is clear that other forms of energy need to fill this gap. How it is possible that demand for refined oil is declining yet consumption is expected to be up by fifty percent (50%)? Someone is not telling the truth. Local resources are the solution to the ever-increasing disparity between supply and demand. Such resources could include: turbine, solar, nuclear, and other not-yet-conceived energy sources.

Further, under my Kingdom's revised departmental mission, access to these sources will be limited by location. Energy may only be obtained within a certain radius of consumption. If your area has a wealth of ethanol-based fuel or if your area has a great deal of coal or natural gas, then your city or town will be powered by all available forms of energy that you have available to your town within that limited radius. When I talk about energy that is gained by powering a city and/or region, I'm referring to energy that powers things like households, factories, and streetlights. The exception to this energy restriction falls with fuel for transportation: energy that powers airplanes, trains, and automobiles.

The federal government will be responsible for the energy grid by coordinating the availability and accessibility of American resources. Under my royal government, most departments will support community programs from afar. However, energy is one of the exceptions as they will be contending with big business (shareholders, investors, oil companies). They'll need the diplomacy to ensure a smooth transition to energy independence; while promoting locally generated development of energy resources in communities nationwide.

Coordination between the agencies

Many agencies have conflicting rules and perform similar duties. Not only will I eliminate overlap, I will ensure that all the rules of the community will be complementary to other departments and agencies. Under my new government, the responsibilities of the Nuclear Regulatory Commission and the Tennessee Valley Authority will be swallowed up by the Department of Energy. I have eliminated unnecessary layers of bureaucracy by moving these agencies to the Department of Energy in order to ensure that all federal agencies with a focus on energy are working in a coordinated manner to ensure we are all doing what is best for the United States in general and installing a sustainable energy plan in particular.

Conclusion

Through the coordinated efforts between my Kingdom's Royal Cabinet Member, Mr. T. Boone Pickens, and the energy industries, my Kingdom will establish an Energy Department that does what it should: develop, implement, and improve upon a diversified approach to ensuring that American communities becomes the primary suppliers of their own energy.

The four main points of my administration's energy department will be:

1.) Develop and maintain an America that is self-sufficient with energy production;

2.) Strive to obtain one hundred percent (100%) of America's energy comes from available American resources;

3.) Utilize the Pickens plan's main tenets of utilizing natural gas and other forms of energy, developing a power grid, and incentivizing individuals to use the most efficient types of energy;

4.) Consolidate all energy-related agencies under the Department of Energy (Nuclear Regulatory Commission; Tennessee Valley Authority

Four: Treasury

I.   Mission Statement

   A.) 2011:   Maintain a strong economy and create economic and job opportunities by promoting the conditions that enable economic growth and stability at home and abroad, strengthen national security by combating threats and protecting the integrity of the financial system, and manage the U.S. Government's finances and resources effectively.

   B.) New: Maintain a strong economy and create economic and job opportunities by promoting the conditions that enable economic growth and stability at home and abroad by protecting the value of the US dollar against inflation, other currency manipulation, which includes implementation of the King's Plan and the United States' legislative attempts at devaluation.

II.   Agencies

A.) Securities and Exchange Commission
    1.) Commodity Future Trading Commission
B.) Banking
    1.) Federal Depository Insurance Commission
    2.) National Community Service Administration
(formerly Small Business Administration)
    A. merged with Farm Credit Administration
    3.) Federal Housing Finance Board
    4.) Export/Import of the United States
    5.) National Credit Union Administration
C.) Retirement
    1.) Federal Retirement Thrift Board
    2.) Pension Benefit Guarantee Association
    3.) National Railroad Retirement Board
    4.) Social Security Administration (privatize)

II. Royal Secretary: Arthur C. Brooks

III. Budget: 2012

A.) Treasury
    1.) 2010: 4% increase in 2012
    2.) 2012: 14 billion
B.) Social Security Administration
    1.) 2010: 11.5 billion
    2.) 2012: 12.5 billion

Introduction

*...I sincerely believe...that banking establishments are more
dangerous than standing armies; and that the principle of
spending money to be paid by posterity, under the name of
funding, is but swindling futurity on a large scale.*
**Thomas Jefferson to John Taylor Monticello,
28 May 1816**

I went sailing, with my family, around the Atlantic Ocean for two and half years from October 2001 through April 2004. After the 9/11 attacks, the markets were dead, the business that I knew how to do no longer existed. Small businesses were being killed by enacting legislation like Gramm-Leach-Bliley (1999) and post-ENRON regulatory legislation like the Sarbanes Oxley (2002). Later on, like other Americans, I witnessed another drain on the market during the mortgage crisis of 2008. I believe this crisis occurred because of the strangle-hold of credit-rating agencies like Amici Moody's Investors Service, Inc. (Moody's) and Standard & Poor's (S&P). These two agencies hold a duopoly held over the credit rating industry and, by extension, all businesses. I needed to leave the business world for a couple years to regroup from these series of business and personal losses.

During that time, I enjoyed life with my family and I began thinking of ways to rebuild our America. Thoughts of retirement troubled me. I knew that Social Security and other welfare-like programs were draining our country's reserve of money as well as America's ability to be self-sufficient. When I returned to land in 2004, I co-founded Sequence Investment Partners. Prior to starting Sequence, I noticed the financial regulations implemented by Congress have resulted in changes that are hurting American small business, which means costing Americans their jobs and stifling the entrepreneurial spirit. As King, with the help of Arthur Brooks, I will change the way the American federal government approaches retirement and the monetary system. Under my Kingdom, the Treasury Department will make several changes that will enrich the economy, boost small businesses, and, balance the Federal budget and temper the nation's debt.

I chose to appoint Arthur C. Brooks because he understands the economic system that will work best for America. He's also made a successful career transition. His first career was as a French horn musician and music teacher in Barcelona, Spain. His wife and he returned to the States in 1992, where Brooks pursued bachelors and master's degrees in economics and a Ph.D. in public policy. He found a home at the American Enterprise Institute because he was "persuaded that free enterprise was the path to the best life for most people."[xxi] His work as an economist has led to his placement as the president of the American Enterprise Institute. He is also the writer of several books, including The Debt, a book about rebuilding the market in the United States in order to develop an economy that is more welcoming to entrepreneurs.

The Treasury Department will take over the Federal Reserve as it currently exists and it will consist of three major sections: the Securities and Exchange Commission; Banking; and Retirement. The Securities and Exchange Commission will include a new agency dedicated to health insurance and it will swallow up the Commodity Future Trading Commission. The Banking Section will include the Federal Deposit Insurance Corporation; the National Community Service Administration (formerly the Small Business Association and merged with the Farm Credit Administration); the Federal Housing Finance Board; the Export/Import Agency of the United States; and the National Credit Union Administration. The Retirement Section will include the Federal Retirement Thrift Board; the Pension Benefit Guarantee Association; and the National Railroad Retirement Board. Initially remaining an independent agency, the Social Security Administration will get unwound over time. Once Social Security has been closed from the realm of government responsibility, all retirement plans will be regulated like any other business under the SEC. The Internal Revenue Service will remain a separate agency limited in scope because of the new consumption tax.

Arthur C. Brooks, my royal cabinet member for the

department of Treasury, will oversee the implementation of the solutions for the financial, insurance, and real estate industries that will lead the elimination of waste, the deregulation of the Reserve, and the removal of ineffective programs.

The six solutions are:
1.) Implement a plan to phase out and shutdown social security;
2.) Take over the Federal Reserve;
3.) Eliminate the credit rating duopoly held by Moody's and Standard and Poor's by opening the industry to other companies;
4.) Reign in Congressional regulation to enable free-market business growth by allowing entrepreneurs and small companies more opportunities to contribute to the development of the American economy;
5.) Ensure that we switch our currency back to the gold standard once we become debt free; and
6.) Ensure that restrictions are put in place for executive compensation.

These six solutions will lead to abolishing the hurdles of over-regulation that are responsible for insufferable slumps in the business, retirement, credit rating, and insurance sectors.

The first category of changes that will be enacted in the federal system of government will involve social services—like social security—that are currently funded by the federal government. These services will be phased out on the federal level. Another category of change will center on retirement planning. These agencies will fall under the Treasury Department. In some cases, states will become responsible for these services; in other cases, they will become privatized. As mentioned above, Social Security will have a multi-phased plan first to be unwound and ultimately to be shuttered. As King, I will start by eliminating the spending we have on social security by phasing out the program.

The final category of change is related to the responsibilities of the current Securities and Exchange Commission (SEC). Under my system, the SEC will fall directly under the Treasury Department. The primary adjustments to the SEC will be to put the rating agencies under their jurisdiction, to open up credit ratings to other companies, and to have oversight of healthcare insurance deregulation. First, the credit rating agency will be placed under the jurisdiction of the SEC. I will abolish the conflict of interest duopoly that Moody's and Standards and Poor's have been given by the federal government. These credit rating agencies have made "freedom of speech" claims when issuing their statements about securities. This claim should be a crime because Moody's and S&P are looked to as authoritative sources on the securities matters, so their speech has a strong bearing on the market. They should and will be held as a fiduciary and, as such, they will not be allowed to just giving meaningless opinions. If they are given more competition, these agencies will be kept honest and they will be more effective.

Deregulation is at the heart of all these changes. By deregulating securities, insurance, retirement, and rating agencies, we will allow America to grow into its fullest potential. One of the first industries that I will have deregulated is insurance. At present, every state government has dominion over which insurance companies can offer services in its state. Any American who likes having options should feel offended by this. There's no reason that insurance shouldn't be offered across state borders. If someone in North Carolina wants insurance, they should have the same services offered to them as someone in Maine. Let the insurance companies come up with the offerings that they want and let them offer it in every state. Of course, consumer protection is still required and we will go after any company and its officers for fraud and misrepresentation. Agents still have to be licensed but if a product is accepted by the SEC it can go nationwide. When telephone service and airline tickets were deregulated, their prices decreased considerably. The same will be true once we deregulate healthcare and other financial industries.

Finally, the U.S. dollar will turn to the silver standard. The new silver standard will be different from the gold standard because Americans can't redeem cash for silver. The federal government will guarantee that we have the silver to back up the currency in reserve. By making this guarantee, the United States currency will have physical value, and the Treasury will print as much currency as we have in silver, eradicating the issue of overprinting and devaluing the dollar. Silver is about forty dollars an ounce, so a dollar will be 1/40 of an ounce. Written another way, there will be a 40-1 ratio of dollars to ounces of silver. With this new standard, the Department of Treasury will maintain in its inventory a 40-1 ratio in silver to the number of dollars available in the public.

With this standard, the U.S. currency will be auditable. The Treasury can prove that they have enough silver in store to cover the availability of cash to the American people. The change to the silver standard will give a lot of psychological value to the American currency without the panic to exchange paper for metal that can occur when markets go bad. When the United States had the gold standard, banks never had enough gold on hand to cover the paper currency. Why silver and not gold? Silver is more functional and it should restrain the printing of money. The Department of Treasury is promising and is accountable to make sure that it has that much available silver.

To maintain the U.S. dollar as the world currency, the United States regulators need to get the Treasury under control. If the Treasury is under control, then Congress is forced to be under control. If the Treasury can't print money haphazardly, Congressmen can't spend like they have been spending because there just won't be enough money to back up their spending. Remember getting a check in the mail for $300 from the Treasury? Think about what you did with that money. What a total waste of tax payer money. The stimulus solution of sending out $300 wasn't even a band aid placed on a gushing wound. Congress must start acting with long term thinking and not just reacting to political pressure. As King, I would find out who originally came up with that idea and send them to the dungeon. We needed to get at the root of the problem by addressing the ways to be fiscally responsible. The government can spark this responsibility in Americans. The $300 band aids were not going to address overspending, under-producing, under-employment, and over-crowded classrooms. My Kingdom will eradicate this wastefulness by rebuilding the infrastructure to reward fiscally responsible Americans.

Retirement & Social Security

Before 1935, Americans, not their government, took care of the poor and needy within their local communities. This care included those who could no longer work because of their advanced age. The viewpoint of pre-Depression Americans was that people who needed support were not the responsibility of the federal government. The town leaders were responsible for taking care of those who needed retirement money. But starting around the Civil War, American's approach to poverty shifted. The country was not prepared for the adjustment needed to support an industrialized, more urbanized population. That shortcoming would ultimately culminate in The Great Depression, was a time when an unprecedented number of

Americans were starving and were in need of financial help. When Franklin Delano Roosevelt made the decision to push the Social Security Act of 1935 through Congress, he created a public retirement plan for those who had aged enough to stop working. Such a plan was more feasible in the pre-Baby Boom generation of the 1930s. Today, it is an outdated policy, and transplanted into modern times; it's setting the government on the path to bankruptcy.

Roosevelt was, without doubt, one of America's greatest presidents, and his ideas worked in the era to which they were designed. But this experiment no longer works. It is now time to phase out Social Security or any retirement plans overseen by the federal government. Retirement should be a private enterprise run by private businesses. Ronald Regan started this process in the 1980s when he established the federal trust fund, implemented an income tax for social security benefits, and raised the minimum retirement age.[xxii] Because I recognize that people have already invested a great deal into their own social security accounts, I have come up with a fair plan to eliminate this welfare program. In my plan, age and net-worth are key factors in deciding how much each citizen will be paid-out of their Social Security investment.

The elimination of this program will be a painful process but as King, I am striving to do what is best for the United States and what will continue to be best for the United States one hundred years from now. It is for situations like America's present malaise that the term "growing pains" was invented. I wish I could make it completely painless, but I can't. Just trust that, like exercise, the pain will be worth it in the morning.

As with any free-market enterprise, some people are going to benefit more than others. Though it's a noble goal, we will never be able to eradicate the class-structure. However, we will be able to empower the people to attain their financial stability on their own. I have two broad categories for deciding how to issue disbursements.

Net-Worth Less Than 2 Million:

The bulk of the population has a net worth less than 2 million dollars. This group of people will fall into this category. What and how the occupants of this category collect will be based on their age. This payment differentiation will be based on whether they are 49 and younger, or 50 and older.

Regardless of wealth, all Americans who are 49 years old or younger will simply receive a full payment of the money that they and their employer have put into the system. They will get a check immediately from the feds, with no interest or compensation. Basically, their payments into Social Security will be considered a free loan to the federal government returned to them without interest. Given our current interest rate environment there wouldn't be much anyway. Once they receive the check, theirs and future generations will be done with social security forever.

Americans who are fifty or older but who are not yet collecting social security will have a different set of rules. As soon as I put this law into place, the government will stop collecting money from this group's income and, by extension; companies will stop matching social security payments.

Each American will be given ninety-days to make one of three choices:

1.) Collect the lump sum of money that has already been put into their social security fund and never deal with social security again; or

2.) Once they are sixty-five years old, they may still begin collecting social security. However, they will collect the amount they would have gotten at a fifty-percent (50%) reduction; or

3.) They may choose to collect full benefits if they and

their employer continue to contribute and decide to start collecting at the age of seventy.

Net-Worth More Than 2 Million:

Any American who has a net-worth between two and five million dollars may choose one of the following options: 1.) whatever age they are, they may take all of the money out that they've put in; or 2.) if they are over fifty, they can stay on the existing plan but at a fifty-percent (50%) reduction. For Americans with a net-worth of 5 million or more, they will not be eligible to get any more social security payments. If they have already retired and they have already begun collecting, they simply stop receiving payments.

Finally, every category that can accept a disbursement or payments will have one final option. Everyone will have the option to decline their disbursement. Should they decline their disbursement; the money will go directly to principal payments on the national debt. Perhaps I'm a starry-eyed optimist, but Americans have always banded together in harsh times, and when problems start to get fixed. I believe many people will choose this path because they will want to do what is best for America.

Payments

The Social Security disbursements are just one way my Kingdom will stimulate the economy. The people that have already put into social security will have to figure out how to reinvest money. Americans will have several options: put the money into IRAs or some sort of qualified retirement account. If they have put in twenty-thousand dollars and they opt to receive a lump sum, they will get twenty-thousand dollars and will have 60 days to either put into a qualified retirement account like an IRA or to spend it.

NETWORTH	AGE	PLAN
5 million+	n/a	Ineligible, lose it
2-5 million	n/a	Take all money put in
2 million or less		Get what promised.
	49 or less	Get all the money back
	50, not collecting	Stop collecting money from income companies stop matching 90 days to make one of the following choices:
		Collect money put in OR same benefit you would have gotten at 50% reduction OR full benefits if collect after 70 years old
	currently collecting	Keep benefit until you die

Chart 8: Chart Explaining the King's Social Security Phase-Out Plan.

If they choose to spend it there will be the 12% consumption tax assessed on the distribution. At that point, the money is theirs and they can do whatever they want to do with it. Because income tax will have been eliminated all money in existing retirement plans taken out early will be subject to the 12% consumption tax. Any American that has accepted, waived, or been disqualified from the final payment will have finished collecting Social Security benefits and the program will end for them.

Any American whose net-worth is less than $2 million that opts to receive a lump sum payment of more than

$50,000 will have to take a class before receiving their money. These classes will be put on by companies that have been certified by the Department of Community Development and Sustainability (Chapter Ten). Private retirement firms will provide the training pro bono because the recipients will likely become new clients. As such, the educational program will cost the federal government and the tax payers nothing. The people will learn how to plan for and successfully enter retirement, and the government will be putting the liability on Merrill Lynch, Smith Barney, and any other qualified broker dealers. These brokers have to be Certified Financial Planners (CFP). In order for a CFP to apply to be one of the approved companies, they need to submit their course curriculum to the Certified Financial Planning Board of Standards for their approval.

Once all the Certified Financial Planners have been established, letters will be sent out to two groups of people who have a net worth that is less than two million dollars and those with over two million dollars. The first group will be Americans under 49 who have given to social security and the second group will be those Americans who are over 50. Both groups will have enclosed in their letters a list of the CFPs who are allowed to teach the class they are required to take before receiving their lump sums. The former group—those who are under 49 and who have a net worth of less than 2 million—will only have the option to receive a lump sum or to lose the money entirely.

The latter group will also have their options explained to them. Again, depending on their net worth, people who have accrued a Social Security account will have the option to either 1.) Accept a lump sum; 2.) be paid at a fifty-percent (50%) reduction when they turn 62; or 2.) be paid one hundred percent (100%) under the existing structure if they wait until turning seventy to collect. Their decisions have to be made within 90 days of receiving the letter, which will be sent by certified mail and the date of receipt will begin the 90 day cycle. If they do not respond, they will automatically have the lump sum as a choice and it will be held without interest until they claim it. If they don't claim it and they die, it is lost. Their estate cannot try to acquire the money.

The citizens who have chosen to receive a lump sum must take the class prior to having the check disbursed. No matter which category they fall under, all lump sum payments will include employer matching accounts. Should individuals who are collecting a lump sum decide that they would like to keep the money without investing in a private retirement account, they will be taxed the 12% consumption tax on the dispersed amount. Further, anyone who decides to take their retirement funds out before they mature will also be charged a consumption tax. The goal is to encourage, not mandate, good saving habits.

Social Security will take as much time as necessary to be eliminated. One might ask when will this elimination happen? When will Social Security breathe its last breath? That all depends on the death of the last person presently over fifty with a net-worth under five million that has decided to opt to receive any social security installment payments (reduced or full). If the last person dies in 40, 50, 60 years from now, that is when the last traces of social security will be eliminated. My plan unwinds and ultimately eliminates social security, the greatest government-backed Ponzi scheme of the 20th century. The federal government will not lose any money and the crime of an unsustainable, overly-expensive public retirement plan is eliminated.

ERISA

Under my government, all federally sponsored plans will be phased out and eventually abolished under similar terms as Social Security. I will encourage businesses to offer retirement plans that are run by private companies.

One such business that helps its employees plan for retirement is Microsoft. Eighty-seven percent (87%) of Microsoft employees are enrolled in its retirement program. This is because the company wants employees to take control of *their* investments. Microsoft employees have three levels of investment portfolios available which cater to how comfortable an employee feels with investing. Microsoft also offers financial education classes. Microsoft is a wonderful model for retirement programs for other American corporations. While my government will highlight their program as a model, my royal cabinet will promote privatization of all retirement programs.

My Kingdom will see the initiation of a new unique benefit with IRA's and 401k's. After I have eliminated the income tax, the deductions and incentives for individual and corporate savings will have gone away. As King, I will instate a new incentive with a rebate on the National Consumption Tax. Individuals with a net worth less than 2 million will be given an incentive to contribute to their retirement funds with this national tax. Depending on how much they contribute to their IRAs and 401Ks, Americans will be allowed a maximum annual rebate of two thousand dollars ($2000.00). The IRA's and 401k's will have the same rules as they do today for distributions with the exception of taking it out early. If you take it out early you will be required to pay the national consumption tax of twelve-percent (12%) on the entire amount. This way, Americans will be motivated to put money into their retirement accounts and leave the money there.

In 1974, the Employee Retirement Income Security Act (ERISA) was passed setting minimum standards for private pension plans. ERISA does not require that employers offer a pension plan. However, it does set a standard for those who choose to offer pensions. Under my new government, ERISA will be modified to ensure that retirement plans will grow tax-free. All of those rules would stay in place for private corporations and government agencies who offer retirement plans, self-directed IRAs, ROTH IRAs, union retirement plans, railroad retirement plans, etc. Although the United States will be eliminating Social Security, it will do so only to serve the best interests of the citizens the governments serves, and that same spirit is the catalyst the government still encouraging companies to have retirement plans. Although income tax no longer exists, there is still a penalty for trying to take money out of company pension plan prior to maturation. Those funds are put together as a benefit specifically for a retirement from that company. Even if you leave the company, the money is matched as a long-term benefit.

The investors in pension funds will still be required to wait until a set age to access the account tax-free and tax-deferred. Companies will continue to contribute matching benefits to employees' retirement accounts. Further, they will begin offering more with retirement packages because these benefits will be more of a bargaining chip for courting high-quality employees. When the private sectors take over retirement packages, they are going to be more efficient than the federal government. It's very important that corporate retirement plans still have to stick with the existing set of rules that apply to employee pensions. By privatizing all retirement plans and pensions, we will take the money out of the crime and the crime will go away. An ideal America is one where Americans will be able to do what's best for the country and for themselves by becoming smarter consumers who plan for their later years.

The Securities and Exchange Commission (SEC): An Agency of the Treasury

The current mission of the U.S. Securities and Exchange Commission is "to protect investors, maintain fair, orderly, and efficient markets, and facilitate capital formation." As King, Brooks and I will make only one change to the mission statement. I will add the phrase "and insurance policy holders" after "to protect investors." This change will reflect the new rules my government will enact related to insurance companies. I will lead the development of the new Securities and Exchange Commission in response to the Sarbanes Oxley, Glass-Steagall, and Dodd-Frank Acts. Further, this section will discuss the virtual duopoly that Amici Moody's Investors Service, Inc. (Moody's), Standard & Poor's (S&P) have on credit-ratings. I will explore answers to the questions: What's wrong with this duopoly and what can be done to improve the free-market and the banking industry in this country? My answer will eventually be: Credit agencies will be held to a much higher fiduciary standard. They will also be unable to use "freedom of speech" to absolve them of the damage their irresponsible speech causes. Freedom of speech is a responsibility, and there is an ocean of difference between being able to say what you like and no being held accountable when you employ your freedom to say what you like to the detriment of others. This is why con men can still be thrown in jail. Before detailing the crime of wasteful spending, ineffective programs, and overregulation resulting from these recent federal laws and the poor-business practices of the credit-rating agencies, I would like to review a brief history of the security and exchange commission, along with the credit reporting agencies.

History of the Security and Exchange Commission (SEC)

The Security and Exchange Commission is less than a hundred years old. This commission was first established by two acts: the Securities Act of 1933 and the Securities

Exchange Act of 1934. The first of these federal laws established a registration requirement of investors in securities in order to prevent "deceit, misrepresentations, and other fraud."[xxiii] This 1933 law set the stage for the Act establishing the Securities and Exchange Commission in 1934. The Securities Exchange Commission was given the power to regulate the principal stakeholders involved with publicly trading securities to ensure that fraud is prevented and punished. In addition to these two important investment statutes, a series of other acts were passed in the 30s and 40s—Trust Indenture Act of 1939, the Investment Company Act of 1940, and the Investment Advisers Act of 1940.

Things remained relatively quiet legislatively until June of 2002 when Sarbanes-Oxley was passed in response to the big Enron scandal of 2001. The goal of the bill was to "enhance corporate responsibility, enhance financial disclosures and combat corporate and accounting fraud." Further, the "Public Company Accounting Oversight Board" (PCAOB) was created to oversee the auditing profession. Sarbanes-Oxley was used to create stricter regulations for periodic and annual financial reporting to enhance the validity (Sections 302, 401, 404) and the timeliness (Section 409) of the reports. The 2002 legislation further established criminal penalties (Section 802) for certain types of fraud.[xxiv]

Sarbanes-Oxley was created in incredible haste by Paul Sarbanes (D-MD) and Michael Oxley (R-OH). It was probably the worst piece of legislation ever written. Frankly, Sarbanes-Oxley's main tenets were already required under 1933 SEC rules. The SEC has decided to enforce some of the sections of Sarbanes-Oxley; while others seem to be ignored. There has been some talk of repealing this ineffective legislation. In fact, in 2010, the Supreme Court ruled in favor of stricter oversight of the Public Company Accounting Oversight Board. In Free Enterprise Fund v.

Public Accounting Oversight Board, the court ruled in a 5-4 decision that the PCAOB had authorities that were too broad. The court went on to state that the Board members themselves were not subject to the traditional checks and balances that come from the Executive Branch. The Supreme Court ruled that the Executive Branch needed more authority over the PCAOB activities. This is one of the many reasons that even though I think we need a temporary king that I remain committed to democracy and the sense of checks and balances we have here in America. In many ways the system works, and in this case the court made a good decision in keeping the power of the PCAOB in check, and hence preventing a monopoly.

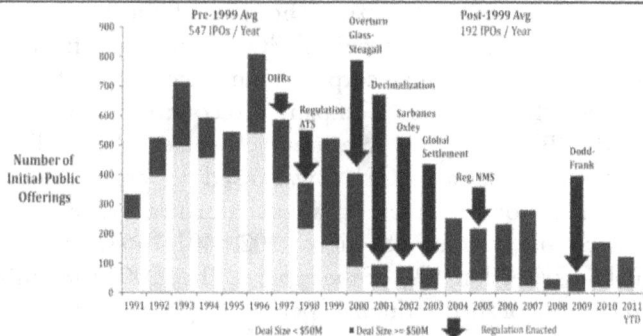

Chart 9: IPOs and Regulatory & Market Changes.[xxv]

Under the leadership of Mary Shapiro at the SEC, the SEC created unsustainable, anti-competitive corporate governance for every company small or large. The downside is the environment that allows for competitive, fair free-market entrepreneurship has been swallowed up by the compliance necessary. Only large corporations like General Electric and Ford could afford the funding required to comply with the reporting rules set in place by Sarbanes. As such, small companies were virtually annihilated because of Sarbanes-Oxley. According to a study conducted in 2011, 311 is the average number of companies that went public every year between 1980 and 2000. Today that number has shrunk to 102.[xxvi]

Sarbanes-Oxley was only good for accountants and lawyers. It doesn't help investor confidence, and it doesn't stop anything on the corporate governance. It simply obliterated the small companies IPO's and by extension the spirit of entrepreneurialism that is the essence of the United States.

The free market economy has all but evaporated because of the regulatory environment. Limiting the free market has been unfair to the small business. When small companies tried to comply with Sarbanes-Oxley, a lot of them went out of business, and you can imagine what that did to the economy upon which every American relies. As you will see in the chart below, the cost to go public has risen to 2.5 million dollars a year; while the cost to stay public is $1.5 million a year. A small company can't afford that astronomical amount; only big corporations like General Electric could survive those tariffs.

The current regulatory environment and credit-rating systems became unfair to small businesses because the only way to get capital was by taking the next step: going public through IPOs. Congress and regulators have made it nearly impossible for companies to raise money to grow their businesses, and America has paid the price for it. The lesson: even though their hearts are in the right place, Congress is out of control with reactionary legislation. Congress enacted Sarbanes-Oxley because of the public outcry resulting from the WORLDCOM/ENRON Scandals, but there are better ways to avoid and mitigate the damage of fraud which do not require other businesses to pay the price for ENRON's crimes. Under my Kingdom, we'd eliminate Sarbanes-Oxley to encourage the growth of free enterprise.

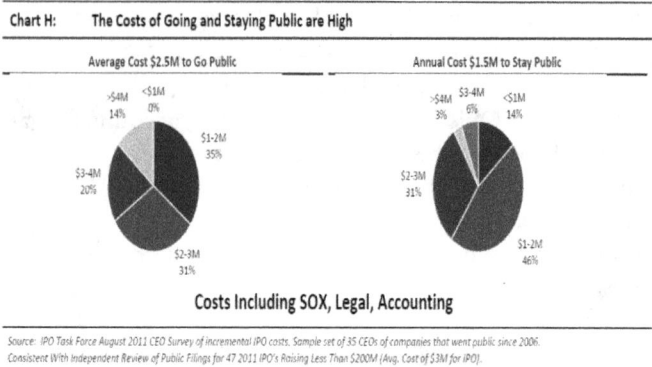

Chart H: The Costs of Going and Staying Public are High

Average Cost $2.5M to Go Public   Annual Cost $1.5M to Stay Public

Costs Including SOX, Legal, Accounting

Source: IPO Task Force August 2011 CEO Survey of incremental IPO costs. Sample set of 35 CEOs of companies that went public since 2006.
Consistent With Independent Review of Public Filings for 47 2011 IPO's Raising Less Than $200M (Avg. Cost of $3M for IPO).

Chart 10: The Costs of Going and Staying Public are high.[xxvii]

Banking & the Securities and Exchange Commission

Modern banking regulation began with the establishment of the national banking system in 1864. The Federal Reserve was created in 1913, which was later amended under the McFadden Act of 1927 that prohibited interstate banking. In 1933, the Banking Act, otherwise known as the Glass-Steagall Act established the temporary Federal Deposit Insurance Commission (FDIC) and separated commercial banking from investment banking. The FDIC became its own agency with the 1935 Banking Act, and its modern responsibilities were established in 1950 with the Federal Deposit Insurance Act. Year-to-Date Activity, 1984 – 2010.[xxviii] Other acts further defined the powers of the FDIC.[xxix]

The Glass-Steagall Act was a piece of legislation that

provided a much needed impetus for the growth of a small business. Unfortunately, the Act was eradicated with the passage and implementation of the Gramm-Leach-Bliley Bill of 1999.[xxx] This was a grievous mistake (and grievously hath American answered for it). Sandy Weill, former Citigroup chairman and executive, made a very brave comment on CNBC in July. He told CNBC's Squawk Box, "What we should probably do is go and split up investment banking from banking, have banks be deposit takers, have banks make commercial loans and real estate loans, have banks do something that's not going to risk the taxpayer dollars, that's not too big to fail."[xxxi]

| Year | Additions | | Total Institutions at Year End |
	New Charters	Conversions	
2010	5	8	6,544
2009	24	10	6,841
2008	90	19	7,098
2007	175	19	7,293
2006	178	12	7,407
2005	167	11	7,527
2004	120	25	7,637
2003	110	18	7,778
2002	90	13	7,890
2001	125	16	8,098
2000	188	22	8,317
1999	228	18	8,586
1998	187	28	8,803

Chart 11: Federal Deposit Insurance Corporation, Changes

He said that it's time to break up the banks.[xxxii] He was calling for the reinstallation of Glass-Steagall, and that is what I intended on doing from the time I began thinking about this book. Glass-Steagall needs to be reinstated in order to bring banking back to the community. As a businessman, my business was greatly affected by the repeal of Glass-Steagall because it changed who I could do business with. With Glass-Steagall, I had the option to raise money through private investors. The post-Gramm-Leach-Bliley environment has led to absurd regulations.

Repealing the Glass-Steagall Act was tantamount to a financial crime that caused the internet bubble and the housing crisis. In response, leading banks became more reckless with their depositors' funds and eventually fell into the dangerous mindset of "too big to fail". After that accountability no longer existed for how they are managed their people and their money. Glass-Steagall had kept things in check for a long time. Now, the United States is going through similar financial woes to those that we went through during the Great Depression.

The repeal of the act has also limited the hard work of America's small businesses, undermining their ability to hire local workers and maintain a reasonable employment rate. As the number of small businesses continues to shrink we are destroying a rich tradition of American entrepreneurialism and ingenuity—both of which have led to our emergence as leaders of the economic, political and social worlds. The Gramm-Leach-Bliley Act allowed the creation of a financial holding company that has the authority to underwrite and sell insurance and securities, to conduct commercial and merchant banking, to oversee other business realms like real estate.[xxxiii] This has encouraged affiliations between banks and insurance underwriters.

Yet another troublesome part (it makes you wonder how such a thing got even a single vote in Congress) of the

Gramm-Leach-Bliley Bill is that financial holding companies are not allowed to conduct business without a "satisfactory Community Reinvestment Act rating." This will be enhanced to fit my concept of empowering communities to address their local issues, including mortgage and merchant banking practices. In the end, these monopolistic banks must and will be broken up.

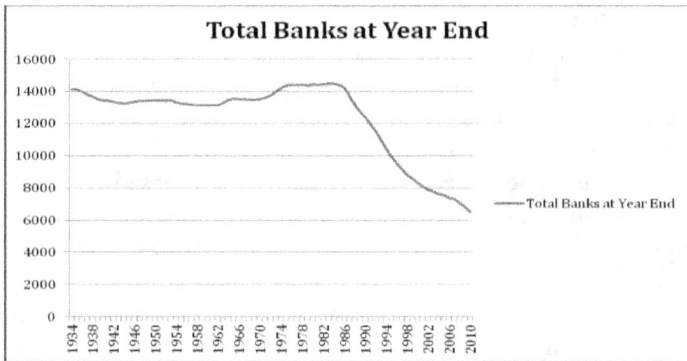

Chart 12: Total Banks in America by Year.[xxxiv]

In 2010, Barack Obama signed the Dodd-Frank Wall Street Reform and Consumer Protection Act. This act changed the consumer protection, trade, credit rating, and financial product regulations. In addition, the act modified corporate governance, methods for financial disclosures, and transaction transparency. While this was an ambitious and well-meaning response to the financial collapse of 2008, the act is not without flaws upon which we can certainly improve. The Act is largely over-burdensome and to comply with it is nearly impossible. Local banks can't comply without almost certainly going out of business. The regulators now have one person assigned to a particular bank. The portfolio investment committee gets together, and as a bank they decide whether or not to make a loan. Because of TARP and Dodd-Frank, one person is given too much power to say yay or nay to loans. This ample authority is now taken away from a private institution and given to one individual who's probably not qualified to really make that decision. Local and community banks are the life blood of small business America. Without the competition they bring, Bank of America can become even "bigger" and even more incapable to fail (at least in their own mind). Now, a bank can only exist if it's a monstrous giant of a bank.

We need to bring banks back to the community in the pre-Graham-Leahy-Bliley Act of 1999. When all of the community banks began consolidation, the lending practices for small business America dried up. Sometimes local businesses were given loans just based on the reputation of the owner. That borrowing/lending power of small business was crushed after all of the banks were eaten up with the repeal of Glass-Steagall. This led to the robo-signing scandal that came to light in 2008 and 2009. Banks would do homework on the company or individual, and because they were familiar with the individual/company they'd override some of the factors which ensure that someone who didn't necessarily fit the computer generated outline of who will receive and who will not receive credit. Instead of using this computer model, they should have been looking deeper into who was borrowing the money and who was making the decision. Dodd-Frank takes the power away from the community, when the power should have been taken away from the machine and given to a local individual. These federal regulators will not fully understand the nuances of the local community, and it will only make things worse rather than improve the local economies.

In the end, banks will be broken down. There should be no such thing as too big to fail. A bank should never be too big to fail; they should be part of the community. Sure, we will have more banks, but we will ensure that we will never have a financial collapse like the one that occurred in 2008 and 2010. As King, with Sandy Weill as my appointed advisor to the royal cabinet, my Kingdom will proceed to break up the banks.

Credit Rating Agencies & the Banking Mortgage Crisis

I firmly believe the entire banking crisis falls squarely upon the methods of the credit rating agencies, Amici Moody's Investors Service, Inc. (Moody's) and Standard & Poor's (S&P). By relying on these two agencies, the federal government created a rating duopoly. Because of how the federal government created this duopoly, they have virtually no competition. The rating agencies were handing out AAA ratings without really assessing the debt, which allowed Goldman Sachs, Lehman, and everyone else to sell all of these subprime mortgages as AAA paper. Yet, S&P & Moody's were unscathed by the crisis. They claimed First Amendment right of Freedom of Speech. Yet, the role they played was much more than that. Their AAA stamp allows for trillions of dollars to trade. Under my system, I would abolish the duopolistic market that these agencies have been granted by the federal government, I would open up the credit rating industry to other competitors, and I would make these agencies responsible for their ratings.

The biggest problem with these credit reporting agencies is how they are paid; by the very brokerage firms that are trying to sell the debt in the first place. If you look at who lost money throughout this whole crisis since 2008, the stock prices of the rating agencies haven't really been impacted. They haven't lost a dime. That is a crime that they have remained unscathed by the very crisis that they had such a big role in causing.

Another change I will make will be in how agencies are classified: I will make all credit rating agencies fiduciaries.

Both Moody's and S&P have issued opinions and then when their opinions have come out wrong, they have stated they were mere recommendations and cannot be held accountable for the outcomes of their recommendations. For example, when Moody's tells Goldman that they think certain bonds should be listed as AAA, Goldman's will purchase (or not purchase) because of Moody's hold on market perception. When that same bond turns out to be deficient in some way, Moody's has hidden under the veil of the First Amendment's right of freedom of speech. They state that it's their opinion and that expressing an opinion shouldn't have negative repercussions—even if that opinion turns out to be wrong. This is another level of the crime. Moody representatives shouldn't collect payment for an opinion and, when the opinion comes out wrong, they cannot get away with saying they are only exercising their right to free speech that should be only used as a reference source. By giving them the responsibility of a fiduciary, we will eliminate the crime of unaccountability for credit rating agencies because we will be holding their credit rating to a higher standard. They will be liable for their advice—good or bad.

To continue along this line, rating agencies failures and incompetence stems also from its impact on the pension fund world. A lot of pension funds can't invest in any stock or bonds that do not have a AAA rating. As such, these agencies should be held liable for wrong ratings. Acting as a fiduciary, their rights of free speech are not comparable to an individual. They are a company, and their opinions hold more weight than a private citizen's thoughts or even a reporter who covers the financial market for the New York Times. Because these two agencies are required to approve a variety of transactions, their opinions should have the same repercussions as an attorney who does not represent his client in the manner that he is expected by law. It is a crime that these two credit rating agencies hold a duopoly and they are not held accountable for their decisions that impact the national and international financial markets.

The level of accountability for credit agencies is beginning to shift. Moody's, S&P and Fitch are all defendants in two sister cases: Abu Dhabi Commercial Bank et al v. Morgan Stanley & Co et al and its sister case, King County, Washington, et al v. IKB Deutsche Industriebank AG et al.[xxxv] The judge in the case, U.S. District Judge Shira Scheindlin, originally heard charges of aiding and abetting fraud, breach of fiduciary duty and negligence and negligent misrepresentation, she has only allowed the last charge to proceed.[xxxvi] Calling their rating methods "negligent misrepresentation," brings them one step closer to taking responsibility for their credit ratings. Sadly, as we learned early in the book, the cogs of bureaucracy turn slowly. In so doing, they have a temporary reprieve the forces of self-interest. It is these forces that have the most to fear from a king.

I contend that Moody's and S&P have a real conflict of interest, and they are a legal duopoly sanctioned by the federal government. Had they had more competition, they would have been more effective. Keep them honest by adding some competition in there. If issuers of debt like Goldman Sachs bring their securities to be analyzed by one of the reigning agencies—Moody's or Standard and Poor— these agencies will attempt to keep the business of issuers by ensuring they receive favorable ratings. The rating agencies do this for pure survival; Moody's doesn't want to lose clients like Goldman to S&P and vice-versa. For example, Goldman may have pooled a group of mortgages together looking for a favorable rating from Moody's. Although Goldman may have submitted only ninety-five percent (95%) favorable mortgages, they needed to be approved en masse. Goldman could put pressure— purposely or otherwise—to ensure they obtain a favorable rating and if they don't get what they want, they will seek it out from S&P who may give Goldman the rating that they want—to lure the business away from Moody's.

The way to solve this problem is by establishing that credit rating agencies rate each mortgage independently. Although time-consuming, this will ensure that mortgages are given a factual rating. However, with this plan, the credit agencies will be drawing on the trust and belief of the mortgage application in the first place. This individualized attention will prevent the inevitable lies that people submit on their mortgages because unscrupulous loan officers have convinced applicants to make up income that doesn't exist. Rating agencies should have identified that no equity existed in the house and that the housing market wasn't going to be infinite. If credit rating agencies look at each mortgages individually and not as a pool, the money will be taken away from the crime. It is obvious why they don't review every single mortgage. The time and energy it would take would make issuing mortgages cost prohibitive.

There are two ways to improve the current state of credit rating agencies; eliminate the duopoly that currently exists by opening the door for other credit rating agencies. Further, make sure they are overseen by an independent board. In order to get accreditation, rating agencies should fall under the jurisdiction of the SEC. Because these ratings affect the market and the market prices of securities, by putting the rating agency under the jurisdiction of the SEC, the rating market is opened up and the playing field is made more level to all parties involved.

Rating industries were asleep at the wheel. Investment firms were buying up notes internally in order to turn around and sell them to investors. These notes were marked up for investors as AAA rated. Firms wouldn't have bought these bad securities if the rating agencies had rated them appropriately. If the firms could have scrutinized Moody's and S&P, they would have passed on the bad securities or at least they would have tried to buy and sell them more appropriately. The same holds true for what happened during the mortgage crisis. The formula that led to the rise in property values in the United States was an unsustainable model. Again, the biggest lessons learned were how the regulatory agencies (SEC, FTC, etc.) were changing the rules for businesses, making it harder for smaller businesses on the one hand, while making it easier for large businesses on the other hand. Under my Kingdom, we will stop Congress's reactionary legislation. Sarbanes-Oxley will be reversed and Glass-Steagall will be reinstated. The banks will be broken up as Sandy Weill suggested. Further, the SEC will be responsible for strict oversight of the credit rating agencies like Moody's and S&P and the duopoly they hold will be dismantled and more competition will be introduced to the securities game as a whole.

Another element of the SEC that will be adjusted relates to the Financial Industry Regulatory Authority (FINRA). Here again is another example of when regulation squashed small business owners' ability to develop their business within a realm of free enterprise. The rules that were enacted limited the number of licensed professional and broker dealers who are permitted to sell securities. The day of the small broker dealer is over. There has been a huge decline in the number of broker dealers because the government has been enacting too many regulations and these regulations make it nearly impossible for a small business to comply. In my opinion, for example, the current head of SEC, Mary Shapiro, is the criminal here. The NASD, under Shapiro, basically bribed all of the small broker dealers in 2007/8. The National Association of Securities Dealers (NASD), self-regulated association that is required for brokers to be a part of the securities business. This is a forced membership akin to union membership. This is wrong.

Prior to 2007/2008, every broker dealer, no matter how big or small had a voice in key votes related to the securities industry. My vote counted just as much as Goldman Sachs'. There were approximately 6000 broker dealers in United States. If you eliminate the top firms, it very quickly went to small firms like mine. The majority of firms controlled the NASD. The NASD orchestrated a way to give a majority of power to very few companies. They merged the NASD with the New York Stock Exchange's regulation committee creating the Financial Industry Regulation Authority (FINRA). Very few firms were members of the New York Stock exchange because it was mostly the Goldmans of the world. The small firms were very happy with the way it was but the big firms needed to find a way to grow and get rid of the competition. The big firms lobbied, for the "good of the investor," to consolidate the two. They created a new system for counting votes that stacked the deck to where a minority of the firms controlled the body. There's no longer a democracy in this organization. The NASD did that by offering every broker dealer approximately thirty thousand dollars to sign up and vote in favor of this change. Total bribery. What small business do you know would turn away an infusion of free capital like that? Instead of granting votes to the majority in the organization, ten firms have dominating authority over FINRA. The vote of small companies has been diminished.

The rules and regulations that apply to broker dealers are becoming so ridiculous and so expensive to comply with that it's putting all their competition out of business. FINRA's squeeze on small broker dealers is another example of killing small business America. Their plan worked to the detriment of America. FINRA has been problematic from its inception, when it was formed in 2006. Being a Self-Regulatory Organization, there was an enormous grab for power by the big broker dealers, and the small broker-dealers were virtually eliminated. As such, the broker dealers sued in the Standard Investment Chartered Inc. v National Association of Securities Dealers. We need to allow smaller broker dealers and other small businesses to thrive in this country.

By reforming the SEC, firing Mary Shapiro, and bringing the small business back to America, we will be doing what is best for the United States. Too big to fail is oxymoronic to the American way. No company should ever become so big and so powerful that they could control and manipulate the good of the people. It's time to bring small sustainable business back to Americans, that free-market, entrepreneurial spirit has been our way of life back since even before we consolidated as a nation after the Revolutionary War.

Insurance Companies: A Case Study for Centralizing in order to Deregulate

The federal government needs to be statutorily responsible for health care. This move to a federalized system of healthcare regulation will be one of the rare instances when regulation will be given to the States. I argue for this federalization of insurance companies because the current system in each state is anti-competitive. Each state has its own set of regulations so every American has different access to different services at different prices. This is an enormous waste.

To highlight this enormously wasteful and unfair system, we simply have to look Blue Cross-Blue Shield. Today, Blue-Cross is authorized to sell insurance in at least 38 states and the company has offices in each state. These "paper-pushing" jobs don't accomplish anything for the U.S. because there is not enough competition. States decide who can and cannot provide insurance in their state, and it's extremely difficult to be among the insurance companies that are allowed to be offered in a state. Each state has its own system of who and what they can and cannot provide; this system is wasteful. The only way to be competitive is to make the entire country open to competition. My changes will reduce expenses because there will be elimination of overlap in every state.

Under my Kingdom, the country will become every insurance company's oyster: insurance companies will fall under the jurisdiction of the Securities and Exchange Commission's federal blue sky law mandated by the Uniform Securities Act of 1956 (USA) and the National Securities Markets Improvement Act of 1996 (NSMIA).[xxxvii] The first act established what an early 20th century Supreme Court Justice termed "blue sky laws." Blue sky laws make it mandatory for all securities to be registered (or officially waived from registration) in the state that the security is offered. While 40 states use federal blue sky laws as the basis for their state blue laws, they vary widely by state. These various restrictions on securities had been prohibitive for the development of commerce. In 1996, the NSMIA addressed this need to regulate certain securities on a national level. When the NSMIA, amended Section 18 of the USA, a class of securities became "covered securities." These covered securities became nationalized and they were no longer subject to the burden of complying to a variety of state restrictions—they are only regulated by the federal standard, in this case the USA of 1953. Right now, any security listed on stock exchanges, mutual fund shares, and other special securities are subject to NSMIA. It is a crime that Insurance companies like Blue Cross/Blue Shield do not fall under the terms set up by Section 18 of the NSMIA. As King, I will include insurance companies and health care products as one of the securities covered by this part of the NSMIA, which will result in a more open market.

To restate, by becoming a New York Stock Exchange-listed company, the IPO doesn't have to file registration statement in each state. If a company's executive wants to go public, they choose to go public in one state and follow that state's blue sky laws. For example, when a company goes public in South Carolina, than then they follow the laws of that state. This requirement is different from any other kind of company. When a company's listed on the national stock exchange, it becomes a part of the federal rules. For insurance, the major states can still have certain things, but must allow national insurance companies to be able to opt out and to not have to deal with states independently. Having health insurance companies follow the same guidelines as companies that are listed on the public exchanges makes a lot of sense.

As any economist will tell you, economics is a game of finding win-win situations. Deregulation of industry is good for the consumer which is of course, good for businesses. When telephone service was deregulated, the costs to the consumer dropped dramatically. Before 1984, telephone companies Pacific Bell and Bell Atlantic held a monopoly over service. This lack of competition made for shoddy service at prices that were too high. Without competitors the "baby bells" did not have the incentive to find better ways to provide telephone service and they could set the prices where they wanted without fear of losing customers. Adjusted for inflation, 1984's long distance service was 51 cents per minute. By 1999, that same service was 14 cents per minute.[xxxviii] Further, studies have indicated that satisfaction with service has increased now that competition breed by capitalism prevails. The same decrease in price happened when airlines were deregulated, with the average air fare dropping by twenty-one percent (21%) from 1990 to 1998.

Competition has been good for airline and telephone service. Sure it's not as easy as having control over everything, but in that scenario the American citizens lose.

With fair competition, businesses and consumers can thrive together, and it will be the same for health insurance. My royal cabinet will oversee a plan that does not make health insurance mandatory. I think mandatory health insurance runs the risk of establishing a monopoly. Under the Sherman Anti-Trust Act, monopolies in a capitalistic society are criminal. My Kingdom will eliminate the monopolies held by current insurance companies and this will lead to cost-effective, improved service. The insurance companies will offer the same prices across the country, and both insurance companies and consumers will not have to worry about being part of groups. By making it a national thing, everybody will be in the same group. This is why every American will pay the same rate.

Because companies will not be paying income tax, they will be more inclined to improve employee benefits and the benefits will be cheap enough for the companies to afford because of deregulation. Employees are still going to demand benefits, and if a business is vying for the marquee employees they will continue to offer a healthcare package or risk losing the potential employee to another company.

Essentially, my royal cabinet will enact changes that will cause health insurance companies to be treated the same as Microsoft and other large companies. They will be required to answer to an advisory board and to fully disclose all company expenditures in annual reports. The SEC will come up with the rules of regulation. These different commissioners will be part of the advisory board to come up with the requirements for each of these policies. One new rule will be a standardization of price to allow all people in the country access to the same services nationwide. That price will be set by the market not the government. The government is merely allowing multiple insurance companies to make such an offering.

The Patient Protection and Affordable Care Act (sneeringly referred to as "Obamacare" by many of the

President's detractors) is a prime example of federal authority with an overreach of Congressional regulation causing financial burdens that have been shouldered by local and state governments. This new law added layers of compliance for every company with more than three employees. Like Sarbanes, this created a system that does not encourage small business growth while also granting more opportunity for work for law and accounting firms. In the case of insurance, this is one example of when Congress should centralize the oversight by giving the Security and Exchange Commission the authority over insurance companies.

With The Patient Protection and Affordable Care Act (PPACA) and under the current system, the consumer doesn't judge the product because insurance will be over-regulated by the state systems. I propose that a licensed insurance agent in each state has to take a test similar to investment advisors from the SEC. My proposal will allow insurance companies to bring a broader array of products for the community to choose from based on what the community needs. Under my new rules, an insurance exchange is going to be created to make health care a legitimate product that can be sold in any state by an agent who is licensed to sell insurance. By creating competition within communities, the monopolies currently held by key insurance companies in each state will be eliminated and consumers will have a variety of products to choose from. A consumer in Alaska is going to have different health issues than a consumer in Florida. Just like other consumer protection labels, there will be an easy-to-understand labeling requirement to show how one product differs from another. With an exchange-traded insurance product, everyone using the product is part of the same group. By mandating that the policies be opened up to everyone at the same price regardless of employment, this will drive the costs down. The bigger the group—the nation as a whole—the lower the cost of insurance.

Insurance agents will be able to offer the same rate for everyone by making insurance company oversight a part of an exchange. The products will be all the same price. A 39-year old female in Alabama will pay the same as a 20 year old man in Utah and a 50-year old woman in Florida. By creating more products, by having a choice of what Americans can buy, the products will be the same price for everyone in the United States.

Further, malpractice and other health-insurance related lawsuits will change. This change will be a whole different set of suing guidelines. Right now, if an insurance company doesn't want to pay, the patient has to go to that state. Under my system, there will be one place to complain: the SEC. If an insurance company chooses not to comply with their part of the contract to supply insurance, that company will be subject to violations under SEC rules. That's not a fun place to be in, so they will be more inclined to ensure that the people are covered in order to avoid dealing with the wrath of the SEC.

Compensation Shifts

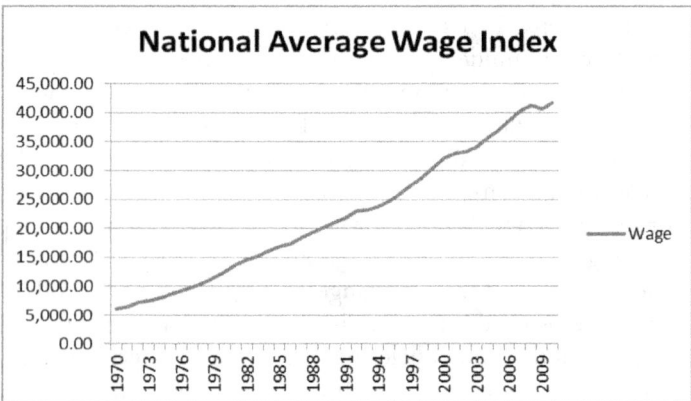

Chart 13: National Average Wage Index.[xxxix]

Executive salaries will never have such a sharp disparity between executive management and the employees. Under my kingdom, I will enact new rules that will put an end to this unnecessarily acute separation. If they are a public company, the executives will not be allowed to make more than 50 times the average salary of its workers. As such, if we look at the average salary as approximately $43,000, then the most any executive in a publically traded company could make is $2,150,000. This would not include unvested stock option grants that are at least 15% out of the money. This is better for the shareholders, better moral for the employees and gives incentive to our public company executives to pay better the lower ranks. For those of you who wondered earlier in the book how I could promise that companies would reinvest profits into their employees rather than hoarding them, now you know.

Figure A4
Median Salary & Bonus Reweighted by Firm Size

Chart 14: Median Salary & Bonus Reweighted by Firm Size.[xl]

With my new plan, the days of executives getting

increasingly higher and exorbitant wages will be over. We will be doing what is best for the United States by taking the money out of the crime.

Conclusion of the Treasury Department

The Department of the Treasury will have some of the most dramatic changes. We are going to develop a Treasury that oversees a revamped banking and retirement industry that will attend to the development of a new silver standard for the reserve. Within this new system, many industries—like the health care system—will be deregulated and made more accessible to all Americans regardless of class-background.

Arthur Brooks will usher in my six essential changes:

1.) Phase out and abolish all government sponsored retirement (Social Security);
2.) Retire the Federal Reserve;
3.) Eliminate the Moody's and Standard and Poor credit-rating duopoly;
4.) Ease Congressional market regulation;
5.) Make the basis of the U.S. dollar to the silver standard; and
6.) Deregulate state-based insurance monopolies; nationwide access.
7.) Inclusion of executive compensation restrictions.

With these changes, we will eliminate all of the should be crimes related to the Federal Reserve and establish a stronger economic system that will lead the way for a better, more sustainable America in which business and citizen no longer feel compelled to work in opposition to one another, but instead will see each other as allies on "Team America."

Five: Defense

I. Mission
    A.) 2011: The mission of the Department of Defense is to provide the military forces needed to deter war and to protect the security of our country.
    B.) NEW: The mission of the Department of Defense is to provide the military forces needed to deter war and to protect and defend the security of our country and Constitution in the most efficient, coordinated, and safe manner.

II. Agencies
    A.) Defense Nuclear Facilities Safety Board

II. Royal Secretary: Lynn Tilton

IV. Budget
    A.) 2011: $531 billion
    B.) 2012: $553 billion

V. History:
    A.) **1775:** the U.S. Army, Navy and Marine Corps were established.
    B**.)** **1790 and 1798**: The Coast Guard and the Department of the Navy were added.
    C.) **1947:** the National Security Act consolidated all branches of the military. Air Force and the CIA were established.
    D.) **1949:** all military had one Department of Defense secretary in the president's cabinet.

Introduction

In Chapter Three, I discussed the establishment of

Oak Ridge City as an example of how the Department of Energy could develop more energy sources. After World War II, the various military installments and camps around the world were dismantled because they were no longer necessary. Much of the military was downsized as the "hot" combat-centric World War II transitioned into the Cold War of the second half of the Twentieth Century. This demilitarization is important because it shows that the military was able to take funding away when the demand for certain programs and bases subsided. Further, military projects like Oak Ridge show the American psyche's ability to pull together in times of great need, and with this collaboration comes moments of great ingenuity for the United States. I believe it's time for the military to consolidate their various platforms in order to work together to eliminate redundancy and ensure that we use military products built in America by American companies.

Five essential changes will make up my royal plan for change in the Department of Defense to reduce wasteful spending, inefficient programs, and over-regulation:
1.) Buy American;
2.) Build American;
3.) Coordinate platforms between the various military branches and organizations;
4.) Eliminate redundancy of supplies, munitions, and other materials; and
5.) Give the decision to declare all wars back to Congress. With these changes, we will bring America back to its rightful place as leader of the free world.

History

The Congress shall have Power To...define and punish Piracies and Felonies committed on the high Seas, and Offenses against the Law of Nations; To declare War, grant Letters of Marque and Reprisal, and make Rules concerning Captures on Land and Water; To raise and support Armies, but no Appropriation of Money to that Use shall be for a longer Term than two Years; To provide and maintain a Navy; To make Rules for the Government and Regulation of the land and naval Forces; To provide for calling forth the Militia to execute the Laws of the Union, suppress Insurrections and repel Invasions; To provide for organizing, arming, and disciplining, the Militia, and for governing such Part of them as may be employed in the Service of the United States, reserving to the States respectively, the Appointment of the Officers, and the Authority of training the Militia according to the discipline prescribed by Congress...

Article 1, Section 8, U.S. Constitution

Ever since the U.S. Army, Navy and Marine Corps were established in 1775 the budget for the military has increased many times over. In addition to the changes of the value of the dollar, this increase in funding is in large part because the needs of the military have changed as the country has gone through various eras (Revolutionary War through the Civil War, World Wars I and II, Vietnam, 9/11, Iraq and Afghanistan). The Coast Guard and the Department of the Navy were added in 1790 and 1798. In 1947, the National Security Act consolidated all branches of the military under the National Military Establishment, replacing the War Department/Department of the Army. That same year, the Air Force and the Central Intelligence Agency (CIA) were established. Each department kept their secretaries, and the CIA was retained as a separate agency. By 1949, all military had one secretary represented in the president's cabinet. Between 1947 and today, the rules of engagement have changed with more advanced weaponry that has included introduction of nuclear power and arms, drone warfare, and a large number of military men and women. The funding for this advance weaponry and military population reflects the needs of such a far-reaching department. In 2011, the Department of Defense had a budget of 553 billion dollars.

One of my essential changes to the Department of Defense lies in the way wars are declared. In Article I, Section 8 of the Constitution, seven clauses are dedicated to the power given to Congress in relationship to war, war departments, and other war-related issues. One of the most debated clauses in this section of Article 1 relates to how Congress gives the president permission to lead the army and, by extension, the American people into war. The President must be granted formal permission by Congress in order to commit our American troops to go to war.

Since 1812, Congress has formally declared war 11 times:
1.) War with Great Britain, 1812;
2.) War with Mexico, 1846;
3.) War with Spain, 1898;
4.) War with Germany, 1917;
5.) War with Austria-Hungary, 1917;
6.) War with Japan, 1941;
7.) War with Germany, 1941;
8.) War with Italy, 1941;
9.) War with Bulgaria, 1942;
10.) War with Hungary, 1942; and
11.) War with Rumania, 1942.[xli]

1942 was the last formal declaration of war issued by Congress. Since that time, the U.S. has engaged in military conflicts in two ways. First, the United Nations' Security Council Resolutions have led us to a number of military engagements. Last, Congress has granted the President special permission to oversee extended military conflicts. While these wars may have had some positive and negative results, they were not how the Constitution intended the United States to go to war. The President's authority is to serve as the Commander-in-Chief, not as the sole-individual who makes the decision to begin military engagements. And our ability to commit our troops to a military engagement has to ultimately be decided by Americans and not leaders from other countries.

King's Changes

I have never been in the military, and I cannot claim to be an expert. However, I have run businesses effectively and at the end of the day, the Department of Defense is a business that needs fixin'. Hence, I have selected a royal secretary, who will make America's military and national security systems more streamlined and yet even more powerful. Lynn Tilton is the best choice for my Department of Defense Royal Cabinet Member. Her qualifications begin with her ability to fix a wide variety of companies which she has demonstrated over a distinguished career. Lynn Tilton is a self-made billionaire who currently owns Patriarch Partners, a corporation that has a central strategy to "rebuild and rebrand iconic American companies and demonstrates a deep understanding for the opportunities that arise in times of adversity and in transformational markets."[xlii] Her skills will support my mission of a more coordinated effort between the different military departments.

Secretary Lynn Tilton has written on her view of how America needs to be rebuilt:

This country has long been a meritocracy founded upon education and work ethic, a nation in which each one of us could overcome the circumstance of birth to live the American Dream. This is not a time in our nation's history for panic, self-pity, entitlement or complacency; it is a time for discipline, hard work and cooperation. Call me naïve, but I believe that faced with the ugly truth, we will roll up our sleeves, raise ploughshares and stand together to rebuild America. xliii

Lynn Tilton

With her passion and energy, Lynn Tilton is going to bring the military into shape. Together we will explore the crime in military spending. This is not to say that military spending is a waste, but even the most committed war hawk cannot deny that the military could spend money better at times.

There appears to be a lack of coordination of supply development between the military powers (Navy, Air Force, Marine, Army, and Coast Guard). Each branch needs to collaborate to ensure more continuity and centralization of gear. This part of my plan, along with some that are to follow, will regrettably eliminate some existing jobs. Remember what I said earlier about growing pains? The effort behind eliminations is two-fold: promoting greater efficiency and pouring the money into educating the workforce for 21st century jobs, such as cyber-security experts, engineers, and economists. We will use the money we save, to ensure American children graduate from high school with a trade that will allow their entry into a sustainable sector of the workforce. Taking care of our troops will be announced by what we do, not just as lip service from our politicians.

The elimination of redundant jobs will not be the only way the military will save money. There are enough others that I could write a whole other book on them. For one, consider that the Navy and the Air Force could be using the same landing gear, using the same contractor and getting a good price so they are not wasting money on different gear, different contractors, and exorbitant prices. There is no disadvantage of having the same kind of parts and thousands of advantages for keeping it simple by using the same parts.

Another opportunity to save is in the realm of research. Right now each branch of the military is conducting similar research and to build similar arms and much of this research is kept secret from other branches. For instance, Naval Research is not privy to the developments of the Air Force. We are all the same country, we are all on the same team, why on earth are we not working together and sharing ideas? Just as energy patents are going to have special cases, we need to ensure all government sponsored research is open-source and collaborative. The military branches represent fingers of the same hand; they should not be working against each other to accomplish research goals.

Another goal of my Kingdom is centered on research development and contractors. Contracts are hoarded right now, and there are all sorts of middle-men in the contracting process. It should be made easier for all companies to be able to sell their products to the military. As such, I will eliminate the concept of the "Prime Contractor". Every company should be given the opportunity to vie for a contract. Further, if there needs to be a Prime Contractor they must be the actual company that completes the work. The work cannot be completed by another company. Of course, there can be subcontractors for big jobs. But I will eliminate the current practice of skimming fifteen percent (15%) off the top and doing all the paperwork, then giving the remaining eighty-five percent (85%) of the funding to a secondary company that does all the work. The secondary company is not allowed to bid independently for a series of reasons not the least of which is that is what has created a prime contractor industry. Smaller companies vie for the attention of the larger, primary contractors and ask the primary companies to bid on contracts. This primary-secondary set-up has turned into a system of bribery, back scratching and cronyism. That's anti-competitive. The secondary company should not be forced to use that prime contractor to bid if they don't have the capability to complete the job. The qualified company should be permitted to bid and win the contract on its own. The way the system currently stands, the subcontractor has to raise prices by fifteen percent (15%) to cover cost to pay the prime contractors. This system creates an additional cost to the tax payer, and we should put an immediate and disgruntled halt to the practice of rewarding those practices.

Another way to make the defense industry more efficient would be to have one central depot for military equipment, vehicles, and aircraft. By doing this, we will have made the various defense branches more unified. There must be one storage unit to which all military branches can turn to obtain supplies. With one agency or hub, and interchangeable munitions and parts, we will be able to trim so much fat off our military. Not only will this benefit the economy through the money we save, it will result in a much more efficient military! But we will need to be able to have interchangeable components for things that we are buying. For example, the Navy's computer systems must be able to coordinate with the Air Force's systems.

Next, my Kingdom will make sure that the military only buys American. For what jobs we lose in the military, more will be created when these jobs are returned to American soil. Our military should never buy airplanes from France, cars from Japan, or any other military equipment from other countries. Our military departments and government agencies in general should be buying from American companies. I can see only two exceptions to this all American rule. Our government should purchase from foreign companies when the product is needed and it is not available in the United States or from an American company. The other instance when the government should buy from another country occurs when the American product is too expensive. For example, if American steel is fifteen percent (15%) more expensive than steel sold by a French competitor, the government should purchase that steel from the French competitor. However, the number one choice should always be to buy American. If we buy elsewhere, there had better be a darn good reason.

With the military buying only products that are built in America by American companies, I see a potential hazard for creating a monopoly. However, although the companies will be collaborating to ensure coordination of parts, they will still be competing for which company gets to make which part. There still needs to be oversight and an advisory board, and the Department of Consolidation and Coordination will oversee this process to ensure that corruption, greed, and mismanagement doesn't occur. To ensure that the contractors and the Department of Defense are doing what's best for the United States.

Finally, all future conflicts must return to what the Constitution has established for declaration of war. The President must have a majority vote granting him approval to lead the army into all future wars. We must not forget the rights laid out in our Constitution, and checks need to exist preventing this President or any future President from forgetting them either. These rights are the essential brass tacks of the United States. Without them our country does not hold together.

The leaders of this country need to ensure that the military protects the totality of America from enemies both foreign and domestic, and they need to be held responsible for ensuring that the country, including the military, does not violate the Constitution.

Conclusion

Under the leadership of my Royal Cabinet Member, Lynn Tilton, will enact changes resulting in a military that is better both for our soldiers and America.

The Department of Defense will become more efficient with the following changes:

1.) Centralize all military systems;
2.) Eliminate all redundancy;
3.) Build military supplies, vehicles, and aircraft in America;
4.) Buy military supplies, vehicles, and aircraft from American companies who build in the United States whenever possible;
5.) Revitalize the process for declaring war as it is written in the U.S. Constitution. Uphold the Constitution by giving the sole authority to declare war back to Congress.

With these changes, I believe the military will become stronger and more self-sufficient. By having a stronger and more efficient military, we will be doing what is best for America.

Six: Justice

I. Mission Statement
   A.) 2011: The mission statement of the Department of Justice reflects the breadth of its responsibility: "...to enforce the law and defend the interests of the United States according to the law and to defend the interests of the United States and its citizens according to the constitution; to ensure public safety against threats foreign and domestic; to provide federal leadership in preventing and controlling crime; to seek just punishment for those guilty of unlawful behavior; and to ensure fair and impartial administration of justice for all

Americans."

B.) **NEW:** The mission statement of the Department of Justice reflects the breadth of its responsibility: "...to enforce the law and defend the interests of the United States and its citizens according to the law and according to the constitution; to ensure public safety and Constitutional rights against threats foreign and domestic; to provide federal leadership in preventing and controlling crime; to seek just punishment for those guilty of unlawful behavior; and to ensure fair and impartial administration of justice for all Americans."

II. Agencies
   A.) Commission of Civil Rights
   B.) Federal Trade Commission
      1.) Postal Regulatory Commission

II. Royal Secretary: Brigadier General Judge James Cullen

III. Budget
2010: 27.65 billion
2012: 28.2 billion

IV. History
   A.) 1789: Established, The Judiciary Act of 1789, Ch. 20, sec. 35, 1 Stat. 73, 92-93 (1789) created the Office of the Attorney General.
   B.) 1870 solidified in its modern form. Congress passed the Act to Establish the Department of Justice.

Introduction

Within arbitration circles, it's known as the American

Rule: the idea that either side of a litigation hearing must pay their own attorney's fees. Virtually every other court system does not have it. Because of it, courts are flooded with overly-ambitious cases seeking much more compensation than to what the person has any sane right and billions are wasted in defendant's attorney's fees.

Plaintiffs and defendants in international disputes are allowed to vie for a particular international or national court as a venue for arbitration to resolve disputes. If it weren't for New York State's exception to the American Rule, it is likely that international commercial businesses would never choose to settle arbitration in the United States. The rules of engagement in New York are different than any other state, and New York has established a lucrative judicial business out of this niche. Unlike the rest of the United States, New York arbiters are allowed to decide who pays the attorneys' fees. In this case, arbiters look at the facts of the case and issue a decision. The arbiter may determine that the Plaintiff pay all, some or no portion of the Defendant's attorneys' fees; and vice-versa.

This rule where the plaintiff may pay the fees of the defendant if they lose does not appear anywhere else in the United States. In America, if an individual or business is sued, they must pay their own attorneys' fees whether they win or lose. This allows someone to inflict financial damage upon a person or an entity that did absolutely no wrong. Aside from being immoral, this is preventing growth because individuals are too busy figuring out ways to sue each other for personal financial gain while other people and companies lose time worrying and doing things to protect themselves for when they get sued. I would love it if, as King, I could be content to rely on people to be honest and fair in all cases on their own. Sadly, this would be an exercise in futility. This type of extortion must stop, and it is up to the government to make it stop. By making plaintiffs pay if they lose, the federal government will limit and eradicate the crime of frivolous and unnecessary lawsuits bogging down the United States legal system.

***

Between 2007 and 2010, the United States Postal Service lost $20 billion, and the debt increased from $2.1 billion to $12 billion.[xliv] A business would not be permitted to continue running with such horrible losses, so why should the postal service? The need for mail services has decreased significantly since the onset of private shipping companies like UPS and FedEx and the proliferation of the use of email and other electronic forms of communication. The United States Postal Service has not kept up with this trend.

Since the Constitution was ratified, Article 1, Section 8 gave Congress the power "to establish Post Offices and post Roads." A series of acts have addressed the changing needs of the postal service like the Postal Act of 1863, the Postal Code of 1872, and the Postal Reorganization Act of 1970. With each act, the United States government has further and further monopolized first-class mail. Prior to 1872, the U.S.P.S. was not using stamps, and they began doing so after a private company had begun using them. After 1872, Congress eradicated private companies' rights to deliver the mail, but not before using the private-company's idea of using stamps. Private business has the freedom of ingenuity that is not always apparent in government organizations.

The postal service is given a slew of privileges granted only to a federal agency. For example, they are allowed to borrow up to 3 billion dollars from the U.S. Treasury. Also, their income taxes pay the income of the postal employees. They also have the power of eminent domain and they are not required to pay parking tickets. All of this is causing more and more of a drain on the federal system.

It is high time that we allow the private businesses the opportunity to bring the postal service offerings into the 21st century. Meaning, the United States has pumped billions of dollars into a failing business that has shown no sign of improving with their current methods. By giving the postal service to a private industry, over-spending on a service that is not working will go away.

***

The elephant in the room when any talk of laws or justice comes up in the political arena is drugs and prostitution, so let's get that out of the way quickly. The Netherlands has legalized marijuana and prostitution. The drugs and sexual behavior are tolerated, even among some of the most religious people in the country. The Dutch do not smoke pot and hire prostitutes as much as the foreigners who visit the nation in the lowlands. Yet, the Dutch ensure protection of the prostitutes and Johns and coffee houses. Further, they obtain a great deal of tax revenue from what is illicit in the United States. The "war on drugs" is nothing more than prohibition was back in the 20's. Keeping things like marijuana illegal has proven to be a costly venture for the United States government. No matter how hard the government tries, people will attempt to participate in these illicit activities. By legalizing marijuana, as an example, the federal government will be able to generate income from the twelve percent (12%) consumption tax, while eradicating the drain these types of cases have on federal courts, jails/prisons, and law enforcement efforts. By legalizing these activities, the money will be taken out of the crime, and the crime will go away.

Solutions

Under my new system's Justice Department, marijuana, and other things will be decriminalized and legalized, the American Rule will be eradicated, and the Federal Trade Commission and the Postal System will be put under the jurisdiction of the Department of Justice. The U.S. will become a better place by nullifying laws that unnecessarily mandate moral issues such as prostitution and marijuana at the behest of large private corporations like tobacco and beer industrial giants. Just to be clear about prostitution, all of the protections must be put into place for the workers. The goal here is to eliminate human trafficking and the abuses these human beings suffer at the hands of evil people. Prostitution and narcotics have an illegal underground business. By being realistic and monitoring it, law enforcement can focus on the legitimate bad guys who are stealing, raping, and killing. Legalizing marijuana will open up a new realm of commerce, while bringing those who have been on the sidelines under the protection and regulation of the laws of the United States. Fewer people will be jailed, killed, and infected; while more people will pay a fair share and give back to the economic system of the United States.

By eradicating the American Rule, we will instill fairness in the legal system for those wrongfully accused solely for extortion in civil and personal injury lawsuits. Finally, the regulation of the postal service and the Federal Trade Commission will be brought under the jurisdiction of the Department of Justice. By eliminating the federal government's monopoly on the postal service, private industry will compete to improve the antiquated, failing system. General James P. Cullen and I will work together to revamp and revitalize the Department of Justice in order to bring it back to working for the American people.

I choose Attorney James P. Cullen because he has

shown time and again the necessary courage to stand up for Justice. Nowhere was this ore on display than during the Bush years, when he worked alongside a group of Flag Officers and human rights groups to stop the torture and interrogation methods used by Donald Rumsfeld and others in the Bush administration. As a retired brigadier general in the United States Army Reserve Judge Advocate General's Corps, he served as the Chief Judge (IMA) of the U.S. Army Court of Criminal Appeals. This experience will allow him an international perspective, as Army attorneys need to interact with American and foreign individuals. I am also certain that he will work hard at making our postal delivery services more efficient, even as we are privatizing the service. Attorney Cullen has worked in construction and real estate law for forty years, giving him an understanding of how to address the issues in the Federal Trade Commission. Today, he is of counsel at the New York Office of Anderson Kill & Olick, P.C.[xlv] The synthesis of his experience in the private and military realms will serve him well as he makes the essential adjustments to the Justice Department. In 2009, he stood behind Barack Obama when the President signed Executive Orders abolishing the United States' archaic policies on torture and interrogation.[xlvi]

His vision proved he is capable of ushering in change and wielding the Constitution to stand in stark opposition to injustice—even when the architect of injustice is the President of the United States.

Marijuana & Illicit Activities

While there have been a moral issues related to the criminalization of marijuana sales and usage, federal organizations like the F.B.I. and Homeland Security and large corporations like tobacco and beer companies have spent hundreds of millions of dollars lobbying to keep marijuana illegal. Marijuana has fewer negative effects than beer and tobacco. More than forty percent (40%) of Americans have tried pot at least once.[xlvii] Further, marijuana arrests make up over fifty percent (50%) of all drug arrests in the United States. These arrests are a sorrowful waste, and they needlessly prevent people from participating in the country's commerce, causing them to instead be an unwilling drain on its resources. Also, you have drug dealers making a great deal of profit off of this drug that is no more harmful than alcohol. Every penny a criminal makes off marijuana is money that would not be subject to some kind of tariff that could support our economy were marijuana legal. In this light, it is clear that keeping marijuana illegal is the *real* crime. We should allow the states to decide on the drug's legality and the federal government should get money by taxing consumers of the drug rather than wasting money on imprisoning them.

While sex for money tends to curl the toes of civil society, the fact is that people will attempt to find sex for pay. People have crossed state and country boundaries just for the thrill of sexual intercourse. During this process, the prostitutes and Johns are put at great risk because of the criminalization of this behavior. Sexually transmitted diseases run rampant, the prostitutes are beaten and murdered, and the Johns and Janes are subject to potential robbery or worse. More than eighty percent (80%) of human trafficking is sex trafficking. By legalizing prostitution, we can protect those who are taken and enslaved to perform this job. This is a crime that any government not bankrupt of compassions needs to legalize prostitution to stop these heinous crimes from continuing. If enough people in a state don't like prostitution, they can make it illegal in their state. For example, California and Nevada should be able to have prostitution, while Utah and Texas may choose to make hiring a woman or man for sex illegal. Communities should be protecting the prostitutes, while generating tax revenue from their services.

In short, the positive economic and social impact for legalizing prostitution and marijuana far outweighs keeping these activities illegal. Regardless of where your morals lie, you must agree that the federal government should be focused on the safety of the people, not on prosecuting what should be a moral wrong. In the end, legalizing prostitution and marijuana and leaving it to the states to decide from there will be what's best for the United States.

Improving the Legal System

The American Rule has led to a lawsuit happy society that allows any money-hungry individual to sue for the most frivolous reasons. My Kingdom will take the money out of this crime of plaintiffs bringing suit by eradicating the American Rule, the unofficial label for the rule that each side pays for his or her lawsuit. I have no problem with any person suing companies or individuals for wrong-doings. If they truly believe they are being wronged, they have the right to have their day in court. However, the legal system right now is burdened with the outright extortion that comes from plea-bargaining as well as the frivolous lawsuits pursuing settlements, and pay-offs. The burden of proof on a frivolous case is far too difficult, which is why most personal injury cases settle. Both sides know that they are going to settle and make some money.

Under my system, this American Rule will be scratched entirely out of existence and I will implement a new rule that states the plaintiff must pay the other side's legal bills should the plaintiff lose the case. This eradication will be a quick solution to the flood of lawsuits currently slowing down the legal system. Individuals and companies will be incentivized to have contingency attorneys for whether they are the plaintiff or defendant. By nixing the American Rule, contingency attorneys will be able to take the case on either the plaintiff's or the defendant's side. To protect against astronomical attorney's fees, when plaintiffs lose, there will be a cap as to how much they will be required to pay. The plaintiff will only pay the defendant's attorney's fees to the limit of what the plaintiff would pay their own attorney's fees. Included in these fees will be expert witnesses and other such expenses. This also includes what they would have normally paid at a reasonable market rate. Opening up contingency to defendants levels the playing field and increases the competition. In order to prevent astronomical fees, there will be a cap on how much plaintiffs will be required to pay.

Eliminating this rule will eliminate the ambulance chasing side of the legal system. This will reduce in a judiciary that is not bogged down by frauds and phonies looking to rip off people who have done no wrong. That's justice, and it's much cheaper and efficient than the system we have in place right now.

The Federal Trade Commission

By incorporating the Federal Trade Commission under the Department of Justice, General Cullen and I will work out ways to deter fraud and to eliminate monopolistic practices.

A major element of the legal system that will be changed has to do with defrauding the system. Any defrauding of the government should be looked at as an act of treason. It's different today. If I steal from Medicaid as a doctor, the harshest crime is a jail-term and/or a steep fine. Under my Kingdom, I will make sure they are punished severely. The rules about fraudulent behavior and the government will be significantly tougher. I will make this treasonous because a citizen must always try his best to prevent fraud against the US. If we simplify everything, there will likely be fewer opportunities and hence fewer instances of fraudulence against the federal government. There will be no more income tax, no reports to file, and no overbilling for more hours than actually worked.

Another more complex goal of the FTC under the DOJ will be to eliminate monopolistic practices. One such monopoly that has to be eliminated is the union-system that has established a strangle hold on a number of industries, such as the postal, police/fire, and educational systems. I will focus on the unions because I think that the unions are an example of a company that has become a state-sponsored terrorist organization. An example of this terroristic behavior happened recently in Charleston, South Carolina, when the National Labor Relations Board filed a case against Boeing for building a manufacturing facility in Charleston that intended to hire non-union workers.[xlviii] The NLRB charged that Boeing was proposing the new non-union factory as a form of retaliation against previous strikes conducted by the company's other union shops. Boeing prevailed in its fight to protect the company's freedom to conduct business as it sees fit within the letter of the law. After receiving a great deal of flack about their role in the case, the NLRB backed off. This Boeing-NLRB case is a success story for free enterprise. However, it has not gone far enough. Randy John, a senior V.P. of the U.S. Chamber of Commerce, lamented, "Although it is a welcomed development that the NLRB is dropping a complaint that never should have been brought in the first place, more needs to be done to prevent this outrageous overreach in the future." An outrageous overreach is an understatement in my opinion. These union shops are terrorizing the local governments and commercial sectors by stalling progress. Another example of unions having too much power happened in the State of Wisconsin in early 2011. All the state congressmen decided to leave the state rather than make the tough decisions needed for budget cuts in Wisconsin.

Indeed, a union has the prerogative to strike. If their demands are not being met, then the people use their strength of numbers to shut down their company. However, just as the individuals have the right to strike, companies have the right to hire non union workers to stay in business and/or move to a friendlier area. The employer should be able to say no without fear of terrorism from striking workers for hiring non-unionized workers. Unfortunately, unions have the power to ostracize anyone who crosses the picket-line and unions have the power to terrorize non-union replacement workers as they attempt to get into the company where the union workers are striking. In a way, this is an echo of prejudice and ostracism of the out group that, in many other ways, rightly died in America in the idle of the latter half of the 20th century. These workers are willing to and able to work, it's very distasteful to watch these hard-working Americans being threatened and spat on by striking workers. It is also hard to watch the striking workers not being paid, while the union bosses make far more than any of their members. This union terrorism needs to stop.

Similarly, unions need to represent all of their constituents and not only the politicians who the leadership sees fit. Unions are taking union dues and using those union dues from their members who are both Democrat and Republican. Without consultation from their members, people at the top of the unions are deciding which candidates that they should be sponsoring and supporting for political contributions. Unions, like virtually all other nonprofit organizations (specifically those organized as a 501(c)3), should be barred from making any political contributions.

The federal government is responsible for ensuring that safety and fair wages are paramount in the way companies do business. In coal mines, auto factories or schools, the government needs to make sure the air is clean, the structures are secure and the people treat each other well. Ultimately, the safety of the populace is the reason governments exist. It is what creates the underlying need for literally every idea in this book. Perhaps most importantly, the federal government is responsible for protecting our American children from the abuses of child labor. When this doesn't happen, the government has failed in the most complete way possible. The government is also responsible for setting a competitive national minimum wage and the government officials are responsible for ensuring that companies do not pay their employees less than this minimum wage. People might work at McDonalds for minimum wage; however most high value jobs will not offer the lowest possible salary to quality, highly skilled workers. People will not accept minimum wage for putting together cars, repairing bridges or teaching our children. The marketplace is going to dictate what that income should be.

Southwest Airlines is an example of a non-union company that treats employees well. Southwest employees are some of the happiest in the airline industry. This company offers a high wage and good benefits without the terror of union brow-beating. Under my government, we will encourage more companies to develop these positive work environments without resorting to the strangle-hold of a union-shop.

Problems with Privatization

Privatization of the postal service must happen as quickly as possible. Unfortunately, eliminating this failing service evokes a fear in Americans that the universal service will no longer be offered. Perhaps many believe that the poor, the rural-inhabitant, and the frail will not be able to receive their mail, and they also sense that businesses might cut corners disallowing delivery to certain less-profitable areas. This fear is a key issue that is holding the government back from opening up the postal service as a private company. However, this fear is manageable. By privatizing, the companies who take over delivery of mail will be beholden to the federal constitution's edict. Should they violate this edict, they will lose their contract. America's constitutional doctrine will make our privatization of postal service even better than other countries that have been successful at implementation.

Germany, Japan, and the Netherlands are among three countries that have shifted towards privatization. Japan is still in the midst of privatizing, however Germany and the Netherlands have successfully moved towards a more modern system of postal delivery. In fact, Germany is looked at as a key success story in the argument for privatization. The Deutsche Post was privatized under the Deutsche Post World Net. Called liberalization of the postal service, or de-monopolizing the federal government's hold on the service, some of the elements of the Germany system that led to their success were, importing managers from other industries, developing new products to offer such as hybrid mail and e-commerce, and modernizing traditional delivery methods.[xlix] All of these new services have been implemented without compromising universal delivery service to all citizens. I doubt anybody can think of a reason why we should expect different here in the United States.

By taking the lead of Germany and what will soon be the system implemented in the European Union, the United States Postal Service will be privatized in order to improve the quality of service by increasing competition. Further any business that takes on the postal service will be made to commit to ensuring universal service to all American citizens. This should allay any fears that any American will be deprived of an ability to receive mail, even junk mail, sadly.

Conclusion

The United States Department of Justice will be brought back to protect American citizens by upholding the Constitution.

This will be done in four ways:

1.) Making marijuana and similarly inexplicably forbidden things federally legal and giving local communities the power to decide if it should or should not be legal;
2.) Eliminating the American Rule;
3.) Incorporating the powers of the Federal Trade Commission (FTC);
4.) Reeling in the powers of the unions under the FTC;
5.) Privatizing the United States Postal Service.

Seven: State

I. Mission Statement: Advance freedom for the benefit of the American people and the international community by helping to build and sustain a more democratic, secure, and prosperous world composed of well-governed states that respond to the needs of their people, reduce widespread poverty, and act responsibly within the international system.

II. Agencies
    A.) Department of Commerce
        1.) Consumer Protection Agency
    B.) US International Development & Sustainability
        1.) US Agency for International Development
        2.) Inter-American
        3.) African
        4.) Peace Corps
        5.) US Trade & Development Agency

    1.) Overseas Private Investment
    Corporation
C.) US International Trade Commission

III. Royal Secretary: Brent Scowcroft

III. Budget
    A.) State
        1.) 2010: 1% increase (not including overseas
        contingency operations)
        2.) 2012: 47 billion increase
    B.) Commerce
        1.) 2010: 5.1 billion
        2.) 2012: 8.8 billion

IV. History
    A.) State department
        1.) Established September 15, 1789
    B.) Commerce Department
        1.) Established in 1903 to report on the
        activities of corporations.

Introduction

Haiti

In early January, 2010, Haiti was hit by a 7.0 magnitude earthquake and a series of aftershocks. The center of this earthquake occurred outside the country's capital of Port-Au-Prince, resulting in mass devastation. The Haitian government reported one million people were affected by the earthquake and at least 316,000 citizens died. The United States, along with many other countries responded to desperate pleas for humanitarian aid. Aside from monetary donations and emergency medical support, the United States aide workers used a different approach to

Haiti. They empowered the people of Haiti by supporting them in a way that allowed the nation to come together and help repair their own country.

According to the Department of State Fact Sheet, the United States initiated a policy that was designed to "foster economic growth, enhance government capacity, and strengthen democracy; help alleviate poverty, illiteracy, and malnutrition; promote respect for human rights; counter illegal migration and drug trafficking; and assist in the reconstruction of the country."[1] These compose the major issues that need to be addressed in Haiti. So, this brings us to the question, how did the United States provide the Haitian Government with the necessary tools to address these issues to become a more independent and stronger nation?

First, the U.S. helped to stimulate the Haitian economy through trade. The Haitian and the United States governments participate in bilateral trade and investment. Haiti exports hand goods and agricultural products; while the United States imports medical supplies and equipment. Both countries benefit from this relationship. In the case of the Haitians, the Haitian people get access to top quality health care products from the U.S. On our end, a U.S. business gets to give back to the world while simultaneously courting a potential future customer. Programs have also been implemented to give people the tools to obtain shelter, employment, health services and education for their children.

Promoting tourism in Haiti is another way that the U.S. helped to boost the Haitian economy without providing direct funds, which would amount to no more than a temporary fix that would be wide open to misuse.

The foreign aid effort in Haiti has played a role of psychological empowerment in developing the country's ability to be self-sustainable. For example, community development has allowed the citizens of Haiti to come together with humanitarians from around the world to rebuild neighborhoods and schools. This has empowered the country to improve its international diplomacy. By including individuals in this reconstruction process, those citizens will know a part of the improvement. They will see that they helped make a difference in their own country and that they played a part in getting their country on its feet, again.

Had we simply handed money to Haiti, temporary relief would have been all that occurred and would promote the idea that more money will always be given to help them. By empowering the people and the government with programs and ideas they can use in their everyday lives, the people are encouraged to go out and help in the cause. Whether by helping with the rebuilding of houses or volunteering at a children's shelter, they see the immediate response to their positive actions. They aren't waiting around for foreign money and volunteers to do the work for them.[li]

***

In 2010, the U.S. supplied foreign aid to countries—rich and poor—to the tune of 53 billion dollars: 38 billion dollars in economic aid and 15 billion dollars in military assistance.[lii] The top ten countries receiving aid were Afghanistan, Iraq, Israel, Pakistan, Egypt, Haiti, Ethiopia, Sudan, Jordan, and Colombia. This aid is granted by five agencies: the US Agency for International Develop (USAID), State Department, U.S. Department of Agriculture (USDA), Department of Defense (DOD), and the Millennium Challenge Corporation (MCC). The top-five low-income economies[liii] received 8.4 billion dollars in aid; the top five lower-middle income nations[liv] received 5.3 billion; the upper-middle income nations[lv] received 2.7

billion; and the upper income nations[lvi] received 263 million. The United States is spending billions of dollars every year to assist other nations. Some of the aid is dire, while other aid is less urgent, even extraneous. In some instances, this funding has persisted and even increased on a regular basis.

As a wealthy, compassionate nation, we should help the suffering, but international welfare must be replaced by programs that fix things for the long haul. We need to establish foreign aid that helps other nations become self-sustaining communities ruled by their native leadership. Even if we were wallowing in complete self-interest as a nation, it's clear that doing what's best for the world is ultimately what is best for the United States. We can't just give someone a fish: we have to teach him or her how to get the fish without our help. To the end of going beyond fixing problems by empowering other nations, as King, I will ensure that all non-military agencies responsible for aid abroad will be turning over their authority to distribute and determine distribution of aid to the Department of State.

Further, American industries have been the masters of branding, and under my government, the agencies of the United States that are responsible for getting aid to other countries will focus on branding American products. We have to market American brands to nations around the world, ensuring that our products have a stronger showing in the international marketplace. This brand-marketing will require diplomacy to promote American products to countries around the world. This goal of international branding is why the Department of Commerce must be moved to the Department of State as the State Department shifts its focus. Building and promoting an American brand will require the best of our diplomacy and it will result in a more favorable image of America around the world.

The United States will become a more independent and self-sustaining country by promoting American brands abroad; by putting the Department of Commerce under the authority of the State Department; and by consolidating all non-military foreign aid responsibilities and agencies under the jurisdiction of the State Department. These three steps will ensure that the United States will intelligently engage in foreign relations in order to distribute aid and commerce. Further, foreign nations will be more equipped to address their issues without the meddlesome hands of nations who use funding as a way to determine foreign diplomacy. We will eliminate international welfare and, in so doing, we will empower third world countries and American businesses together.

Brent Scowcroft will be appointed to serve as the State Department's royal secretary. His abundant military and diplomatic service abroad makes him an ideal candidate. He has already served as a close-advisor to the president with his service as National Security Advisor to Gerald Ford and George H.W. Bush. His work for the Air Force has spanned a series of positions. After he graduated from West Point, Scowcroft was a jack (and master) of many trades in the Air Force: he taught Russian History at West Point, served as Assistant Air Attaché in Yugoslavia, headed the political science department at the Air Force Academy, and served in the office of the Secretary of Defense International Security Assistance. His numerous accomplishments as a civilian reveal a man equipped with a vast knowledge of how to negotiate commercial business on the international stage. As Vice Chair of the international consulting firm, Kissinger Associates, Scowcroft began his international work as a civilian when he "advised and assisted a wide range of U.S. and foreign corporate leaders on global joint venture opportunities, strategic planning, and risk assessment."[lvii] According to the Scowcroft Group website, his other international experience comes from his master's and doctorate in international relations from Colombia and his work as the

Chairman of the Foreign Intelligence Advisory Board and as a member of the United Nations Secretary-General's High Level Panel on Threats, Challenges, and Change. [lviii] His ability to gain respect from international entities are canonize in the form of honors from European nations like the Honorary Knight of the British Empire (K.B.E.) and the Grand Cross of the Order of Merit of the Federal Republic of Germany.

His work at maintaining and developing a business like the Scowcroft Group will serve him well as the U.S. Department of State transitions from one centered on giving aid to one centered on empowering countries to be self-sufficient. Scowcroft's ability to raise awareness of America's mission abroad will translate nicely as he begins to promote American brands on the international stage.

Solutions

Foreign Aid

Several agencies will be consolidated under the Department of State. The United States Agency for International Development will be renamed the International Development and Sustainability Agency. Their new mission will be to coordinate and balance the needs of various regions around the world. This mission will be done in a way that supports the humanitarian goal of democracy and civil rights. The new International Development and Sustainability Agency will have oversight authority of the U.S. Agency for International Development, the Inter-American Agency, the African Agency, the Peace Corps, and the U.S. Trade and Development Agency (which will swallow up the Overseas Private Investment Corporation). The U.S. International Development and Sustainability Agency will also ensure benefits for underserved community groups and small enterprises as well as for promotion of American objectives abroad. Finally, the agency replacing the USAID will provide immediate emergency assistance to countries suffering from disasters with the goal of making each country return to self-sufficiency at the earliest possible date.

To this last point, I want to ensure that emergency aid does not turn into permanent aid. Even if the straight up gift of money were the best way to help nations recover, that would not change the fact that our coffers are finite and so is our ability to give. The aid that we give must have an immediate and urgent goal of ensuring that the country returns to being self-sufficient. We must realize that "recovering" means a return to independence in a better state than before. We'll be helping these unfortunate nations to the best of our ability by allowing them to be powerful enough to continue day-to-day governance and policy without the crutches of foreign aid. If they can't figure out how to live in their own country without foreign aid, then the population should be forced to shift to a place that is sustainable rather than persist in places that cannot sustain communities. Haiti marks an example of when the United States was on the right track to scaffold in necessary changes and to remain poised for full withdrawal once the country had enough strength to stand on its own.

Foreign Policy

Under my Kingdom, U.S. foreign policy will be focused on state-to-state diplomacy and international trade and commerce that promote American ideals and products around the globe. The US International Trade Commission will have oversight of the US International Development & Sustainability. This agency will ensure that all aid and trade are still fair, equitable, and commercially viable.

I am sure that countries around the world will be very

concerned and upset about our new self-sufficient foreign policy at first. But all economists realize that these kinds of shifts happen all the time as nations ebb and flow in how much they export vs. how much they import. The fact that we want to rely more on our own homegrown products does not mean we will not still be contributing to the global economy, only that we'll be contributing in different ways.

Program	Post-War Relief Period 1946-48	Marshall Plan Period 1949-52	Mutual Scty Act Period 1953-61	2010
I. Total Econ. Assistance	107,094.9	138,788.0	152,199.3	37,670.6
A. USAID & Predecessor	.	107,975.9	107,507.4	14,068.6
B. Agriculture	.	581.3	39,801.4	2,637.9
C. State	.	.	.	12,224.3
D. Other Econ. Assistance	101,117.2	30,230.8	3,756.0	5,836.2
E. Voluntary Contributions to Multilateral Organizations	5,977.7	.	1,134.5	2,903.7
II. Total Military Assistance	3,872.8	72,437.3	123,215.7	15,057.6
III. Total Economic & Military Assistance	110,967.7	211,225.3	275,415.0	52,728.2

Chart 15: Summary of All Countries; Obligations in millions, constant 2010 $US[lix]

For example, Saudi Arabia will not be happy with the fact that the U.S. will be instilling a culture of energy independency and sustainability. China will be another country that will surely give us some diplomatic flack. How do we work with China to let them know that our debt and currency will be less dependent on their products and supplies? Their leaders will have to make adjustments, as we are taking back our fiscal independence. Saudi Arabian and Chinese diplomats will have to strike a fair trade with our country. If they want to sell us their products, there should be an equitable balance of imports and exports. This is a perfectly reasonable expectation for the United States. The problem is that it has been the other way for so long that it feels bold by comparison.

On the other hand, the United States should resume trade with countries that have been banned from participating in trade with American businesses because they are considered undemocratic. Cuba is the primary example for trade that should resume. By not giving them money, we are banishing them. Banishment should only be applied when a country poses a national threat—like America's reaction to Iran's current nuclear posturing. Cuba poses no national threat to the United States. In fact, by opening the borders to tourism, their economy will have a boost and the people will eventually turn on the dictator.

Commerce Agency

I love America, so whenever I acknowledge the crime of callousness in our foreign policy it is always with a tremendous amount of sadness. The crime stems from working with business worldwide that promotes human rights violations like employing child laborers in Africa, human trafficking of Eastern European women, ecological travesties like chopping down rain forest in Brazil, and dishonorable business practices like putting lead paint on toys in China. We must stop rewarding this unethical and criminal behavior by issuing aid to these countries. The State Department's responsibility will be to create a dialogue with countries to discuss how the aid policy will affect them and how we can increase brand usage in other countries in the world. We will explore how we can work together as a society, apart from the people dangerously bereft of empathy. To prevent dissonance, Brent Scowcroft will tour the globe, meeting with the leaders of every country to discuss the new method of distributing aid.

This is one reason of many why the Department of Commerce will now fall under the jurisdiction of the State Department. The Commerce Department's main goals these days center on creating and analyzing the census, promoting American business at home and abroad, applying standard weights and measures, and issuing patents and trademarks. The new mission of the department-turned-agency will be focused on economic growth, sustainable development for all Americans by working in partnership with businesses, universities, and communities around the world. The agency will be responsible for promoting the American economy through national and international development of technology, entrepreneurship, business development, and environmental stewardship.

The Commerce agency will work with corporate American entrepreneurialism to support American commerce in order to help corporate America sell their goods and services at home and abroad. It will coordinate with communities to provide consumer protection. Whatever we promote as American brands, we must ensure, for the sake of our own credibility (not to mention our own integrity) that these products are sold accurately and safely to the buyers. The Commerce Agency, under the State Department, will be the liaison with other countries to help American products and services to be sold and marketed to other places outside of the United States in a way that not only promotes our goods, but in a fashion that establishes America as one of the most honorable nations with which others can work.

The Commerce Agency will have a central responsibility for the development of a free market for American goods outside of the United States. This agency will also protect the intellectual property of United States' citizens, companies, and government agencies from the piracy of rogue nations. This piracy protection will include protection from stolen software, music, handbags and more.

The best governments are the most honest and the most steeped in compassion. We will have a global responsibility to show and model good practices. We will show the most ecologically sound methods for drilling a well. We will protect consumers around the world from faulty American manufacturers who choose to knowingly sell unsafe products. If products are banned in the United States, the company may not sell that same product abroad. Therefore we will strive to make it so that the highest standards will be those of America, and company on earth will know that it is to our standards their products must ascend for their business to thrive.

The way to improve America's brand abroad is to promote sustainability in other countries. We will market our brand of ideals and products, but also encourage other country's sustainability while modeling and promoting ethical business practices at home and abroad. We will never profit at the expense of our soul.

Conclusion

The State Department's new mission will be promoted by Brent Scowcroft to countries around the world. His work will be to change the image of America and of American companies so that we are approached with trust rather than skepticism. Scowcroft and I will implement a foreign aid policy that will encourage empowerment of individual countries, while ensuring that the United States is not being taken advantage of when it comes to foreign aid. By promoting the development of local commercial and industrial markets in countries around the world, we will encourage our own sustainability as well as the independence of foreign nations.

The best way to improve the world is to encourage a sustainable, economic environment. The best department in the country to accomplish this goal is the Department of State because they have already made the network to access the key players in this transition.

To make the changes in the State Department, my government will take steps to do what's best for American Foreign Aid, Policy, and Commerce:

1.) Eradicate unnecessary aid;

2.) implement a system of weaning countries off of American aid through the newly implemented United States International Development and Sustainability Agency (formerly USAID);

3.) Implement a plan for marking the American brand on the international marketplace under the newly defined Commerce Agency;

4.) Increase funding to promote Americans studying abroad.

Under my Kingdom, the American brand will become more popular and more coveted than goods made in China. All of these steps and methods will be doing what's best for Americans and American business by taking the money out of the crime. These steps will eliminate the crime of overspending on projects in foreign countries that are not necessary for the development of the American market.

Eight: Labor

I. Mission Statement
    A.) UNCHANGED: To foster, promote, and develop the welfare of the wage earners, job seekers, and retirees of the United States; improve working conditions; advance opportunities for profitable employment; and assure work-related benefits and rights.
    B.) NEW: To ensure the workforce is educated to fit contemporary needs, to guarantee the safety of our workforce, and to prevent abuse in America's workplaces.

II. Agencies
    A.) Department of Education
    B.) Equal Employment Opportunity Commission
    C.) Federal Labor Relations Authority
    D.) Federal Mine Safety & Health Review Commission
    E.) National Mediation Board (Mediate Labor Disputes)

III. Royal Secretary: Jack Welch

IV. Budget:
    A.) Department of Labor
        1.) 2010: 12.16 billion
        2.) 2012: 12.8 billion
    B.) Education
        1.) 2012: 77.4 billion

V. History:
    A.) Public Law 426-62: An Act to create a Department of Labor – March 4, 1913

Introduction

In 1913 William Howard Taft signed the Department of Labor Organic Act, establishing a new department dedicated to fostering, promoting, and developing "the welfare of wage-earners of the United States," to improving "their working conditions," and to advancing "their opportunities for profitable employment."[lx] He signed the bill under protest:

> I sign this bill with considerable hesitation, not because I dissent from the purpose of Congress to create a Department of Labor, but because I think that nine departments are enough for the proper administration of the government, and because I think that no new department ought to be created without a reorganization of all departments in the government and a redistribution of the bureaus between them. The distribution of bureaus between the existing departments is far from being economical or logical, and if there is one thing that is needed in the present situation it is a reorganization of our government on business principles and with a view to economy in the administration of the regular governmental machinery. I forebear, however, to veto this bill, because my motive in doing so would be misunderstood. There is a provision in the bill itself for a recommendation by the head of the new Department as to the reorganization of bureaus that may itself lead to a general reorganization which is so much to be desired.[lxi]

Essentially, Taft signed the Department of Labor Organic Act as a compromise. He wanted to ensure that the government would be revamped in order to bring the government process to his modern era in 1913. He wanted to develop fewer rather than more departments,

My new Department of Labor would have a different focus. I would move four agencies to Labor: the Equal Employment Opportunity Commission, the Federal Labor Relations Authority, the Federal Mine Safety & Health Review Commission, and the National Mediation Board. The Department of Education will also be folded up and will become the responsibilities of the Department of Labor.

The new Labor Department will make sure that our people have opportunity through education. They will ensure that Americans, both young and old, are guided on an educational path that will allow them to learn the skills necessary for jobs in the 21st century.

Safety will be a major tenet of the new department with agencies like OSHA regulating business and factory environments to ensure the companies are keeping their employees protected from potential health and safety hazards. Finally, they will no longer be responsible for retirement and pensions, as these privileges will be privatized under the Department of the Treasury.

Below are main ways that the Labor Department will change.

1.) Include the Department of Education to focus on preparing the children to become a part of the workforce.
2.) Eradicate all unions. The National Labor Relations Board will also be eradicated.
3.) The Equal Employment Opportunity Commission will eradicate quotas based on race, ethnicity and other arbitrary factors. Instead, companies will be encouraged and free to hire the most qualified applicants. American companies will still be punished for encouraging racism. However, companies will no longer be forced to keep an

ineffective worker because of the fear of litigation for wrongly termination based on race.

4.) The Federal Labor Relations Authority will have duties similar to the Office of Personnel Management. They will recruit, hire, train, and fire government employees.

5.) The National Mediation Board is an agency that has now become obsolete because the railway is now federalized. Their responsibilities of oversight of the railroad disputes will be taken over by the Federal Labor Relations Authority.

In this chapter, I will focus on the implementation of the first three goals. To accomplish these goals, I will appoint Jack Welch. Mr. Welch has proven to be a preeminent leader in the global community. Welch began his career at General Electric, remaining there for more than twenty years. In 1981, he became the company's 8th Chairman and CEO. In 2000, Welch was named Manager of the Century by Fortune magazine. This tenure prepared him to be the royal secretary for the Department of Labor. Further, his reputation as a severe manager with a frequently polarizing approach has earned him the name Neutron Jack. Welch is essential for his partial use of his Six Sigma's, which promotes the concept of putting departments under scrutiny to either "fix it, sell it, or cut it." In terms of the government, Welch's selling will become consolidate it, privatize it, or eliminate it. The Department of Labor will need someone like Welch to enact the five essential changes I have planned for this department.

Education:
Preparing a 21st Century Workforce

Congress established the U.S. Department of Education (ED) on May 4, 1980, in the Department of

Education Organization Act (Public Law 96-88 of October 1979).

The mission was to:

> ...promote student achievement and preparation for global competitiveness by fostering educational excellence and ensuring equal access. It engages in four major types of activities: Establishes policies related to federal education funding, administers distribution of funds and monitors their use; Collects data and oversees research on America's schools; Identifies major issues in education and focuses national attention on them; Enforces federal laws prohibiting discrimination in programs that receive federal funds.

With my royal government, the mission of the Education Agency within the Department of Labor is to educate our population to the highest achievable standard in the world by promoting student achievement and preparation for global job competitiveness. So many problems facing America today would be little more than history if every man and woman were educated, so it will be our goal to make educating equally accessible to every man and woman. We will do this by supporting states and local community educational achievement programs. The agency will still engage in the four major activities at its bedrock. However, the second activity will be reworded to include the positive achievements of high-performing schools and districts by identifying and focusing national attention on major issues and opportunities in education

The current education system is set up to promote unrealistic expectations for children. Moving forward, curriculums will be portfolio-based and they will have a strong focus on fiscal responsibility. Further, students will not be shipped to another neighborhood in order to learn.

Methods used by Saul Khan and Bill Gates will help Jack Welch to determine how to approach revamping our education system.

Many of the same tenets and educational standards given to the adults who went through financial training before obtaining the social security education will be given to high school students. Every student will be required to open a checking account in order to learn how to manage finances while still in a safe environment.

It's time for the focus of education to shift to fiscal responsibility rather than pie-in-the-sky dreams that are not very likely to come to fruition. Having a better math and science and art program is more important than having a good baseball team. Right now there seems to be a trend of eliminating art and band, math and, science. This is not looked upon as a good thing. Everyone wants to be a star: there is too much of a focus on how Johnny can be a millionaire baseball player. It's time to shift by giving the responsibility for education to the state with a mandate. In order to receive funding, the state needs to come up with a plan. Every plan will be different: the Alabama plan will not look the same as the Arkansas plan. This is how we're going to best educate our kids. We need to extend a competition between the states and the needs of the labor market. Schools should not be hyper-focused on SAT scores or other standardized tests. They should be focused on guiding children to financially viable professions.

An example of where this is working the Charleston Charter School for Math and Science in Charleston, South Carolina. Charleston charter school is an example where the kids are learning and doing amazing things. This is the kind of school that needs to be funded and supported.

Another example of good education practices is one that focuses on financial literacy and development. Some private schools are already teaching students about how to access the market and how to approach personal banking.

For example, a New York Times article highlighted the class taught at Westover School in western Connecticut. The class is run by the non-profit, "Invest in Girls." This program combines classroom lessons, field trips, and mentoring with financial leaders. This program is preparing our children to go into the professional world with the financial sense to be mindful and careful with how they spend and save their money.[lxii] Instead, we currently have students going into the world with a frivolous and sometimes less than basic understanding of how to use money wisely. The Department of Labor will be responsible for helping bridge local school systems with the financial leadership in their community.

Another element of education that has been a tradition in many parts of America is shipping students to another school system. Under my Kingdom, this system will be eliminated. Unless parents are paying for private school, students in public secondary and public elementary education systems will be required to stay within their school district. Indeed, Brown v. Board of Education ensured that separate but equal was no longer allowed. However, if you choose to live in a neighborhood, you choose to send your children to the schools in that neighborhood. To ensure that communities are getting equal access to the funding, states will need to step in and mandate distribution of the funds. School systems have traditionally been town-by-town fiefdoms. The states can help to eradicate such disparities by distributing funds in a fair manner. The states will have to ensure that each town has equal access or they better be prepared to explain why there is a difference in funding. For example, maybe there is a need for an archery program in a rural community and maybe there is more of a need for an understanding of urban politics in the city. The state will determine the fair distribution of funds for these different programs.

Again, it is ridiculous to move the kids. Even when

you move the kids, the schools are still troubled and you are making the kids go somewhere that the family did not choose to live. Don't move the kids, fix the schools and fix the system. How will states know what is working? They can get a little help from the federal government. The Department of Labor will highlight the programs that are working. The incentives will need to go the smartest states.

These days everyone gets a trophy—trophy for effort, trophy for first place, and a trophy for last place. Enough. Giving everyone a trophy, regardless of ranking and ability, will end with my reign. Everyone is different, and there will always be both sharp and dull tools. Instead of creating an overt sense of self-confidence, we need to help kids find, understand, and enhance their strengths and weaknesses.[lxiii] There will be kids who understand how to make it to the top and there will be those trying hard who are never going to feel comfortable with the academic courses. Children need to be aware of their potential jobs and professions. They need to be presented with the pros and cons of being a doctor, salesman, and all other jobs. Some children will not be able to vie for the professional world. This is where trade schools need to come into play. The way I see it, children who graduate high school have two possible paths: go to college with a focused intent to have a job at the end or they need to graduate with a certification in a particular trade. In order for children to have realistic goals, they need to be presented with an education path that will get them employed. This structure will strengthen our colleges and universities because they will be accepting children that want to be in a university.

The goal for this new structure of education will be nothing short of the maximum we can achieve: ensuring one hundred percent (100%) employability for all of our high school, technical school, and college graduates. Schools will have a stake in ensuring their graduates have jobs, as the federal government will give money to schools that have proven they have excellent graduation and employability rates. School administrators will maintain records of achievement for the students after they graduate so they know how to make adjustments to prepare the students for the workforce in their state. If they are educating a whole bunch of teachers and mechanics and there isn't enough demand for these jobs, then they need to adjust how they are educating the students. If they need more scientists and lab technicians, then the school system had better be structured to ensure the development of interest in these fields.

I hope to see an enrichment of the spirit of entrepreneurialism. This country was founded on the craft of entrepreneurs and we must make sure our progeny are ready to take up that torch and run farther than we could have ever dreamed. Our history is filled to the brim with free thinking people who have come up with new ideas and who have established businesses. Since America's early days, these ideas and businesses have been behind job creation.

Finally, the core curriculums will be based entirely on making practical, self-sustainable adults. Right now we are creating a lot of high school graduates who don't know how to balance a checking account, how to make a resume, and how to behave in an interview. The school system must have a structure in place that requires mandatory classes on money/banking/finance and classes on how to land a job. By the time my Kingship has ended, one of the requirements for high school graduation will be to have a checking account and to have gone to a job interview.

Portfolios, Not Testing

Standardized Testing is a crime in our education system. The time it takes to "teach to the test" takes away from the value of applied learning in the Arts and Sciences.

Science and technology are always growing and changing in our world. Jobs are always available in these sectors. America will always need doctors, scientists, computer technicians, and engineers. The jobs of the future lie in these fields. By taking time away from these subjects, educators are putting our children at a huge disadvantage. They are not preparing them for prospective occupations. If we want to give the youth of our nation a fair chance to effectively and successfully participate in the job market both locally and on a global scale, we need to look at alternative testing. Portfolio testing is the way to ensure that the American education system is developed in a way that sustains a strong and viable workforce.

According to Peter Henry who published *The Case against Standardized Testing,* 11 million exams were added in elementary and middle schools in 2005 as a result of public concern regarding the quality of high school graduates. Henry goes on to explain that these high-stakes tests consist of multiple choice questions that focus on lower level thinking. The questions on these tests do not challenge students to be creative, analytical, or to work as groups to problem solve. Yet these are the skills necessary for the jobs of today and tomorrow. Jobs that require a lower level of thinking are being outsourced abroad because it is cheaper. There are limited job opportunities for Americans with this type of education.[lxiv] In order to rectify this problem we need to be educating and testing our children in a way that trains them in the use of higher level thinking such as analysis, synthesis, creativity, and collaboration.

This is why portfolio-based assessment is the best way to bring America back. Instead of one test full of multiple choice and short answer questions that neither challenge nor show a person's depth of knowledge, let's organize a year's worth of student work in a portfolio. Show where the child began and ended. Show those long term projects such as designing the strongest bridge in science class and writing a research paper on how to stop global warming in English class. Let the children show what they can do, which will be useful in the growing world of science and business. Let them become more knowledgeable in subjects that will aide in their future careers and let them show how they can be valuable assets to our society. Taking education into their own hands gives young people the type of confidence needed to empower them and to help them believe that they could become viable contenders in the American and global job market.

Not only do portfolios allow children to show their work, but they are also given the opportunity to reflect on the process. One important aspect of portfolio-based assessments is that students ask themselves what they can improve on as individuals and note where they are struggling. They are taking ownership of their work and are not just learning facts and figures, they are learning self-reliance. This is a lifelong skill that will be beneficial to their future careers where they must continuously think how to improve on the projects on which they are working. The money we are wasting on standardized testing could comprise a clinic on inefficient spending. It is not effective at ensuring that our children are on the path to getting jobs. Not only is the system of standardized testing ineffective, it actually has the deleterious effect of creating a gap between the haves and have not's.

This money could be, and should be going to improving the curriculum in science, math, technology and the arts. All of these are subjects that are needed to prepare the youth of our country for the global workforce that is developing. In order to promote higher level thinking necessary to strengthen America's workforce (and to ensure that our future leaders, which will one day be comprised of today's students, are making educated, informed decisions), it is important to challenge our children by strengthening the Science, Technology, Engineering and Math (STEM) subjects. By assessing students through portfolios rather than tests, we are able to determine the thought that went into individual projects and tasks, as well as assess our students in a way that asks them to determine their strengths and weaknesses without having that analysis handed to them by a teacher.

I would appoint Bill Gates, founder and CEO of Microsoft, as an advisor to advise Jack Welch in the Department of Labor. Gates understands the future of the American workforce, explaining that each year; the computer science field grows by 100,000 jobs. In order for the American youth to be prepared for this high demand career, "we must demand strong schools so that young Americans enter the workforce with the math, science and problem-solving skills they need to succeed in the knowledge economy."[lxv] Gates goes on to explain that encouraging schools to promote project-centered education is the way to improve the quality of education children are receiving in the areas of math and science. Gates adds, "If we are to remain competitive, we need a workforce that consists of the world's brightest minds." Starting with the way children are taught and preparing them for job opportunities that are in high demand is the way to allow America to remain competitive in the global marketplace.

Salman Khan would also be appointed as an advisor, specifically as the second education advisor to Royal Secretary Jack Welch. Khan is the creator of Khan Academy, a virtual school where students can view videos to help them understand concepts in mainly math and science. On the math side, these videos range from basic addition through calculus. It is this type of individual approach to learning that can benefit students in any grade level from elementary to college. In theory, a teacher could have a class of varying learning levels while teaching the same concept to all children. Each child would start their virtual education at a different level, and teachers could monitor each of the students, assisting those who require extra support. It is this type of student-centered education that will give each child the skills necessary to succeed in school. Khan states of this type of schooling, "The Khan Academy could operate a one-room schoolhouse, where students use our material to get core skills in math, science, grammar and vocabulary. Once they complete their work, they would have the rest of the day to build robots or write stories or take pictures."[lxvi] In essence Khan is providing kids with the skills they need to succeed in math and science and then providing them with time to explore where these skills may take them in their future careers. They are actually getting the chance to put what they are learning to use in project-form.

Gates and Khan approach the education of the youth in different ways, but both share the attitude that our schools are lacking in the way that they educate. Although they may disagree on approaches, they have both been successful with their educational methodologies. For the regional specialization inherent to my educational system, this will be an ideal pairing. For instance, Khan's methodology may work more for Alabama, while Gates' approach may work better in California.

Unions

The 2008 General Motors bailout marked another dangerous shift in American history. It marked government intervention in a market that should have healed itself. Instead, the federal government stepped in and kept plants open that should have closed. They were aided in this effort by the vocal protests of the union workers of General Motors. Progress sometimes means that older businesses, companies, and industries must shut down to make room for new ideas, businesses, and industries. By obstructing the natural process, the President and the GM union protesters unwittingly obstructed progress.

General Motors keeping open failing factories because of the bullying practices of the unions is just another example of why unions must be stopped. If the unions didn't have a strangle hold on General Motors then GM would have been able to adapt long before the crisis and they wouldn't have needed a bailout in the first place. At the time of their inception in the 19th and 20th centuries, unions served a very important purpose. Back then unions helped workers access rights like fair wages and safe work environments. However, now that these rights are part of the governmental system, unions are no longer in the best interest of the United States.

Unions aren't working for what's best for the country because they have excessive terrorist tactics and they are anti-competitive. If a company operated like a union, the attorney general would be down that company's throat. Unions are de facto companies. Union and or non-profit organization executives should not, in any sane universe, be able to make more than 5 times the average employee or members, whichever is less. Because they get funding from the public and its' members, it's clear that unions are public companies. On the other hand, a private foundation is not public unless it takes donations. If a company is private the executives can take whatever salary they want.

Further, employees will no longer be required to join the union to get a job, so I will be eliminating union-only shops. After that, companies will be able to hire the best people and union and non union employees can work side-by-side. It will be the employees' choice, just like any other benefits offered by the company. Employees will no longer be forced to do something that they don't want to do. Also, government unions will be outright banned.

Unions will be treated the same way we treat public companies and will fall under the jurisdiction of the SEC. As such, the government will have a hand in what the executive compensation is for public companies, unions, and non-profits. The executives for unions and non profits will not be allowed to make more than 5 times their average employee. That means that if the average employee makes $35,000 a year, the executive can make no more than $175,000 a year. It is unfathomable to me that union heads today make millions of dollars on the backs of our teachers. This change is the only way to ensure that executive compensation gets back in line and is fair.

This is not to say that unions have never been useful, that would be false on its face. In the late 19th and early 20th century unions fought to ensure that child labor was eradicated, to make certain that people were given a fair wage for their labor, to increase the safety and protection of the people working for companies, and to shorten the work week and work day to forty hours and eight hours respectively. These changes to the workplace and the workforce were all positive. I cannot negate that such changes wouldn't have happened without the pressures put on companies and the government to come up with solutions to these problems. But even then unions have always had that official and unofficial link to corrupt organizations like the mob. However, this tradition of safe and fair workplaces has now become a part of the American way and there should be little concern that the country would return to the pre-20th century world of destitute and unsafe conditions for workers were unions to be taken out of the equation. Like wisdom teeth in humans, unions have become a vestigial appendage to the United States. They once served us well, but nowadays they are a cramping pain and need to be removed. The Department of Labor and other agencies within the government will see to it that they are.

After all, that was the original purpose of the Department of Labor: to ensure the safety, the well-being, and the quality of life of the workforce. Unions are no longer needed with the Department of Labor available to ensure violations are not occurring. Unions have become abusers of their power with their bosses flying in private jets and taking enormous salaries and benefits. They are virtually state-protected terrorists who bully individuals who will not become part of their organizations as well as extort unrealistic and anti-competitive compensation and benefits from companies. As such, I will eliminate union-only shops and, eventually, I will eradicate all unions.

Equal Opportunity Commission

I know this will be an unpopular statement, but it's not the first shocking idea in this book and you've made it this far. Besides, it seems to me that most revolutionary ideas, though common as grain now, began as unpopular statements. The idea that African Americans and women should be allowed to vote, for instance, were wildly unpopular at the time. We only have the today because people were bold enough to voice them. So here it goes....

Affirmative action needs to be eradicated. I do not believe that affirmative action is helping anyone in the country, *especially* minorities. If anything, it has further created a division of entitlement and disgust within the workplace. In the pursuit of fairness, we must stop forcing companies to hire unqualified people simply on the basis of race and ethnicity. The automatic assumption that people should be sued for firing someone because they are a minority is ridiculous. If the person is doing a poor job, then they should be fired. This preferential treatment is not helping minority people become more viable workforce contenders. Rather, it's hurting them because they will be perceived as staying on the job with substandard performance only because employers are afraid to fire them. The fear of having an employee who cannot be fired for a lacking performance has actually resulted in employers being reticent to hire minorities. This is wrong. Employers should have equal ability to hire and fire any of their employees, and they should not fear hiring minorities.

Frankly, being forced to hire non-qualified people based on race makes the company non-competitive. People should be considered solely on their education and experience. Because the Department of Labor will be making education better, every American citizen will one day have equal preparation before entering the workforce. By having an educational system that is focused on employability, this problem of racial disparities in the workplace will be eliminated and everyone will be given a fair shot based on the quality of their ability and character; not on the basis of arbitrary factors like skin color, religion, and ethnic-background. Level the playing field on the educational level, and ridiculous laws like affirmative action will not be needed. Human Resources employees should only be discriminating based on experience; and affirmative action sets up a system that allows inexperienced and unqualified people to have jobs just to fill some arbitrary and unreasonable quota. As such, affirmative action will no longer be permitted under my Kingdom.

Conclusion

The Department of Labor will focus on preparing a workforce for its contemporaries through an education with an eye towards employment and safety. We want to ensure that our labor pool is employed and they are employed in a safe and non-abusive work environment where employees work appropriate hours and are not coerced to do things through immoral means. The changes in Labor will be accomplished by educating our students and adults to be prepared to fill the needs of the modern workforce, by eradicating the unions hold on our country's psyche, and by eliminating affirmative action.

Nine: Homeland Security

I.   Mission Statement:

    A.) 2011: The Department of Homeland Security has a vital mission: to secure the nation from the many threats we face. This requires the dedication of more than 230,000 employees in jobs that range from aviation and border security to emergency response, from cyber security analyst to chemical facility inspector. Our duties are wide-ranging, but our goal is clear - keeping America safe.

    B.) NEW: The Department of Homeland Security has a vital mission: to secure the nation from the many threats we face, to coordinate and collect data from all relevant security agencies (DOD, CIA, DIA, FBI), to help local law enforcement and the FBI to keep America safe, to provide timely and accurate information regarding internal threats to the United States, to ensure that the nation's fast, safe, efficient, accessible and convenient transportation system meets our vital national interests and enhances the quality of life of the American people, today and into the future.

II. Agencies

    A.) Transportation

    B.) Federal Maritime Commission

    C.) National Railroad Passenger Corporation

    D.) Selective Service Commission

    E.) Transportation Security Administration

III. Royal Secretary: Peter Thiel

IV. Budget 2012
  A.) Homeland Security
       1.) 2010: 42.891 billion
       2.) 2012: 43.2 billion
  B.) Department of Transportation (now part of DOH)
       1.) 2010: 12.3 billion
       2.) 2012: 13.4 billion

Introduction

If the Department of Energy was tasked with coming up with a plan to maintain America's independence by eliminating the country's reliance on foreign energy sources. The Department of Homeland Security is charged with protecting this move from national and foreign interests by constitutionally limiting the powers of the U.S.A. PATRIOT Act, by incorporating the responsibility for developing a transportation system that supports this mission of sustainability, and by discouraging companies from hiring illegal immigrants through heavy fines placed on the managers.

Peter Thiel will be appointed to serve as the Royal Cabinet Member for the Department of Homeland Security. He is a self-made billionaire who was the co-founder of PayPal, which he sold to EBay in 2004. Thiel understands technology and has conceived of a myriad of ways to advance our cyber-infrastructure. His mentality will jive very well with my royal cabinet, as he understands the importance of allowing people to pursue reasonable career paths. Recently, he offered twenty grants of one hundred thousand dollars each for individuals who would be willing to take two years off college and work to explore their professional capacity outside of the school environment. He is totally willing to stick his neck out for us. As the Secretary of Homeland Security, Thiel will ensure that the coordination between all facets of national security is further enhanced. His ability to build business and fix ailing businesses will be applied to the DOH, where he will ensure sustainable transportation with our new energy policy, protect these plans from possible manipulation or malice from foreign interests, and ensure fair immigration policy and practice that punishes the executives and managers who violate America's laws.

Patriot Act Powers Reeled In

...I want to know how far you will go
to protect our right of free speech?
because it only took a moment
before it faded out of reach...

Ricky Lee Jones, Tell Somebody
(Repeal the Patriot Act).

The U.S.A. PATRIOT Act would have been well-served to have been subjected to the line-item veto. The Act has reached far beyond the needs of national security that were pressing in our post-9/11 world. We should not be compromising of our liberties and rights. Fighting terrorism is a very important issue. However, preserving what makes this country great is also very important. Without those liberties, what are we defending from terrorism in the first place? The charge of Homeland Security is to safeguard these liberties while not going overboard to implement protections against attacks on our homeland.

Transportation

Under my government, the Department of Homeland Security will work closely with the Department of Energy to protect the interest of American companies in developing homegrown energy and forms of transportation. In the event that foreign countries and their energy companies respond to the nationalization of America's energy plan negatively, the Department of Homeland Security will be poised to protect the American companies involved in safeguarding this newfound mission of self-sufficiency.

One way that Homeland Security will ensure the stability of the new energy plan will be to swallow up transportation-related agencies. The Department of Transportation will be demoted to an agency within the Department of Homeland Security. As a part of this shift, the Department of Homeland Security will swallow up the Federal Maritime Commission and the National Railroad Passenger Corporation as well.

Twenty-percent (20%) of all diesel fuel in the United States is used by tractor trailers. One major policy will be to convert all American trucks delivering interstate goods will be required to run on natural gas. The department will implement incentives to convert all air, land, and sea vehicles to natural gas. By working with the communities to solve their transportation issues, states and local communities will solve their specific transportation needs and problems. For example, Alaska needs to deal with shipping in the arctic, while Oklahoma will have to focus primarily on trains, planes, and automobiles. T. Boone Pickens' proposal for the greater use of natural gas in heavy duty trucks and fleet vehicles is included in NAT GAS Act (H.R. 1835 and S. 1408) and the American Power Act.

To encourage energy independence, the Department of Homeland Security will encourage all trucking industry vehicles to convert to natural gas. This will have an immediate and noticeable impact. Centralizing the trucking industry's vehicles will get the Environmental Protection Agency off their backs. Right now every engine is slightly different and the trucks have to go through a million dollar test that the EPA requires, and there are thousands of engine-types that utilize various fuel types. The goal is to streamline a cost-effective way to provide assistance to the trucking companies to convert all of their trucks to natural gas. The DOE, Peter Thiel and I will focus on trucks that deliver goods along the major routes. By focusing on these main delivery sources, the new policy of converting all trucks to natural gas would have an immediate effect on gasoline prices for the consumer. Finally, we will put a flat tax on gas. Like all other products, we will have a twelve percent (12%) consumption tax for all fuel, foreign or domestic. There will be one exception to this rule: we will implement a consumption tax that is half that rate on natural gas for 2 years and then escalate up. That means that natural gas will be taxed six percent (6%), incentivizing consumers and industries to buy vehicles that run on natural gas. We will be motivating this nationwide switch from gas to natural gas through positive, rather than punitive, taxation.

The best way to ensure we convert the trucks on the major delivery routes to natural gas is twofold. First, we must build an infrastructure where all commercial licenses utilize natural gas. The second point is to offer zero interest rate loans to filling stations and trucking companies to fund the additional expenses that will be needed to convert their existing equipment to natural gas. Because there is no infrastructure to rely on, the Environmental Protection Agency is fighting the conversion and this fight has manifested itself with road blocks to converting existing engines to natural gas engines. This new measure will solve both problems.

By coordinating with the Department of Energy, the Department of Homeland Security will build a national network of transportation energy needs, coordinating with the DOE goal of energy independence and sustainability in the U.S. If we consider the Manhattan Project, the folks at Oak Ridge, how quickly they all fell in line to ensure the creation of a new source of power; nobody can doubt that we could achieve incredible things in the present: like coming up with a plan that allows us to rely solely on energy produced at home.

Natural Gas Consumption Tax Exemption	
2013	6%
2014	6%
2015	8%
2016	10%
2017	12%

Chart 16: Natural Gas Consumption Tax Exemption.

As with the Department of Energy, Homeland Security will work to build the natural gas infrastructure and create jobs by converting automobile and other vehicle engines to compatible with natural gas. This oversight will be to change the fleet of tractors trailers and other national vehicles to a dependency on natural gas.

Immigration

Before the United States was even established as a nation, immigration had been a part of the history of this land from the time of Christopher Columbus. Over the years, our policy on immigration has changed, usually shifting based on the economic and political conditions of the country. In the beginning, immigration was encouraged and the immigrants served the role of pushing our economy through the end of the Industrial Age. This changed in the late 19th and early 20th centuries as Jewish, Italian, and Asian immigrants came to the United States. In response to these new immigrants, the leaders of this country put in place more restrictions on who could and who could not come. The United States encouraged a relatively open-door policy until the Immigration Act of 1920, which determined quotas on the number of people who could come from each country. Today, we have a strict system in place that centers on preventing illegal immigration, only allowing a certain number of people to enter the country from foreign nations. The Dream Act has gotten so much attention these days because it is clear that our current method for addressing illegal immigrants is not working. However, the Dream Act is only paying lip-service to the problems arising from illegal immigration; it is more about politics and elections. The Dream Act and other measures that prioritize political posturing over effective legislation will be eliminated by my qualifications amendment that limits reelection terms for Senators and Congressmen. Every federal politician will only have one weapon with which to fight for reelection: their voting record.

To date, we have spent billions of dollars to unsuccessfully prevent and stop illegal immigration. Because of our new tax structure, we will be able to collect money from all people who live in this country. As things stand, America has been losing approximately 2.3 billion dollars in income tax revenue.[lxvii] With my new system of taxation, every consumer will be contributing as a tax-payer to the American economy whether they are a visitor or a citizen. Our current policy on immigration does not work because we are going after the poor individuals who usually work very hard to help support their families back home. However, I think this is a mismanagement of funding. Our focus should be on penalizing the companies and not the individuals. Let the people come and spend money. If they want to work, let's make the process easier and work with companies to make them legal. My royal cabinet and I will ensure that CEOs and managers who hire illegal immigrants without making them legal face criminal charges, and the hard working people who are currently in the U.S. will have an easy pathway to citizenship and/or work permits.

Families are broken up when one or two individuals are found to be illegal. Children are put into foster care and parents are estranged from their children. This is a crime against compassion, and if we take the money out of the crime it will go away. If we put all the penalties and blame on the businesses that are persecuting these needy people then the personal tragedies surrounding our current system of illegal workers will come to an end. Those who have been working in this country for more than ten years will be given a speedy path to citizenship. This is a fair offer to individuals who have committed to working for an American company, asking them to leave after that much time is not only callous, but with the Consumption Tax in place it will take away a valuable contributor to our economy.

It's an unfathomably absurd piece of bias that corporate America has no real, meaningful penalties for hiring illegal immigrants. By focusing on deporting people, we are merely siphoning the problem to another location without ever solving it. When Americans complain about these people taking their jobs, they don't stop to think that the jobs occupied by illegal immigrants are generally the type that Americans don't want, which is why these jobs tend to be in high-demand (construction would be one example). Allowing the immigrants to fill these jobs contributes greatly to productivity. If they are willing to work hard, why should someone is forced to hire someone who works less hard because they had the good fortune to be born here? After my rule, these workers will be protected by the DOL. Productivity is what's best for the United States. By being an educated, healthy society, we can stand as a nation that the rest of the world looks to for inspiration, guidance, and leadership on humanity-based issues like immigration.

We will also continue to allow and encourage foreign students to come to study in the United States. However, they must get money from their home nations. Right now we are spending millions to pay foreign students to come to the U.S. We should instead be paying our own students to study abroad. Non-American students are still welcome to come and study at our top-notch universities, but we're not going to pay for it. This goes back to training our children for a viable job in the 21st Century marketplace. This question of how best to ensure that our kids can have jobs that are above minimum-wage will be explored in further length in part three of this book.

One side note on this topic, I am making English the official language and, like Europe, making learning a second language required in our schools. If people immigrate to our country, they need to find a way to communicate. One requirement to become a citizen will be to pass a spoken English test. This is an economically powerful step. If we can all communicate with each other, we can hear leaders, politicians, management, workers and more. By communicating in a common language, by de-criminalizing the immigrants, by criminalizing hiring illegal immigrants, America will become a better place.

History

In the wake of the terrorist attacks of 9/11, the Department of Homeland Security was established in November of 2002 to serve as an oversight agency to ensure that all information related to national security was centralized. From its inception, Homeland Security has focused on improving national coordination between agencies. While not perfect, from John Ridge to Janet Napolitano, the department will serve as the exemplary for my new agencies.

September 11, 2001. The date conjures up images of plumes of smoke from the World Trade Center in New York City and the Pentagon Building in Washington, DC. The acts of terrorism that morning showed America that we aren't as safe from a homeland attack as we had assumed. Immediate action was needed to prevent something so devastating from ever happening again. Eleven days after the attacks, Governor Tom Ridge was appointed as the first director of the Office of Homeland Security. This office became an executive department in 2002 under The Homeland Security Act.[lxviii] For the first two years of this act, the department did its best to prevent terrorist attacks, to reduce the vulnerability of the United States, and to assist in the recovery from such attacks.

In 2005, more than 250 members of the department participated in a review where these members would realign the department to increase its ability to prepare, prevent, and respond to terrorist attacks and other homeland emergencies. The results from this review were soon tested. In 2006, Hurricane Katrina hit the Gulf Coast. The result was catastrophic damage to not only towns and businesses, but to the lives of thousands of people. As a result of this event, President Bush signed into law the Post-Katrina Emergency Reform Act. This act established new positions within the Department of Homeland Security to more effectively handle kindred disaster to Katrina.

In 2010, Secretary Janet Napolitano led the completion of the first-ever Quadrennial Homeland Security Review (QHSR), which established a unified, strategic framework for homeland security missions and goals. The results of this review brought to light what the department was doing well and what improvements were needed. On the positive side, the Department of Homeland Security had created new positions and programs to ensure that America was being protected on different levels (cyber terrorism, illegal immigration, natural disasters, etc.) Constant reviews since that time have also helped to strengthen the department. Another upside to the DHS is its physical structure. The department is made up of more than 22 individual offices, which allows many aspects of homeland security to work together as a unified entity. When many individuals, from different expertise are involved in a common goal, it can help strengthen the department.

The chart below, taken from the Quadrennial Homeland Security Review further explains the various reasons we need the Department of Homeland Security.[lxix]

Threats and Hazards	Global Challenges and Trends
• High-consequence weapons of mass destruction • Al-Qaeda and global violent extremism • High-consequence and/or wide-scale cyber attacks, intrusions, disruptions, and exploitations • Pandemics, major accidents, and natural hazards • Illicit trafficking and related transnational crime • Smaller scale terrorism	• Economic and financial instability • Dependence on fossil fuels and the threats of global climate change • Nations unwilling to abide by international norms • Sophisticated and broadly available technology • Other drivers of illicit, dangerous, or uncontrolled movement of people and goods

Chart 17: Reasons Justifying Establishment of Homeland Security.

Although the department has made great strides, it is not done growing yet. The General Accountability office has received reports that show where improvement can be made. The sharing of information needs to be improved upon. Reports indicate that cyber-based threats are occurring more because such information isn't being shared within the necessary departments expediently enough. There are also management issues that need to be worked out in order to ensure that money is being used appropriately and effectively when carrying out missions. A financial management system has yet to be established at the DHS. I'm sure everybody reading this book can guess at how favorably that hits me. Lastly, the General Accountability office notes that there is limited strategic and program planning resulting in a lack of efficiency when it comes to managing threats. Improving these three areas of concern could strengthen the department.[lxx]

Conclusion

In Part Two, I have reviewed already existing departments and listed how they will change under my Kingdom. Along with Malone Mitchell (CDS) and David Camp (DOC), my Royal Cabinet is as follows: T. Boone Pickens (Energy); Arthur Brooks (Treasury); Lynn Tilton (Defense); Brigadier General Judge James Cullen (Justice); Brent Scowcroft (State); Jack Welch (Labor); and Peter Thiel (Homeland). These cabinet members will all work together to achieve the overall goal of encouraging the country's redevelopment by eradicating wasteful spending, eliminating ineffective programs, and promoting deregulation across the federal government.

The goals of the departments are summarized below:

1. Energy: Three major goals to achieve sustained energy independence in America:
   A.) Pickens Plan: use natural gas and other energy sources, develop an efficient and effective power grid, and incentivize

individuals to use the most efficient types of energy
- B.) Consolidate all energy-related agencies
- C.) Make American one hundred percent (100%) energy independent
2. Treasury: Implementation of seven solutions that will lead to abolishing over-regulation:
- A.) Phase out and terminate social security and all other federal government-sponsored retirement plans
- B.) Unmake the Federal Reserve
- C.) Open up credit ratings to other companies by eliminating the duopoly held by Moody's and Standard and Poor
- D.) Reign in Congressional regulation to enable American businesses to grow in a free-market that allows for entrepreneurs and small businesses to be enriched by and to contribute to the development of the American economy
- E.) Ensure that we switch our currency back to the silver standard
- F.) Deregulate state-based insurance monopolies and open the borders to insurance companies
- G.) Implement new public company executive compensation rules
3. Defense: Implement five main goals of the Defense Department:
- A.) Centralize all military systems
- B.) Eliminate all redundancy
- C.) Build military supplies, vehicles, and aircraft in America
- D.) Buy military supplies, vehicles, and

aircraft from American companies who build in the United States whenever possible

E.) Revitalize the process for declaring war as it is written in the U.S. Constitution. Uphold the Constitution by giving the sole authority to declare war back to Congress

4. Justice: The five main goals of the Justice Department are:

A.) Make prostitution, marijuana and comparable things that are presently unlawful federally legal and give local communities the power to decide if they should or should not be legal.

B.) Eliminate the American Rule

C.) Incorporate the powers of the Federal Trade Commission (FTC)

D.) Reel in the powers of the unions under the FTC

E.) Privatize the United States Postal Service

5. State: The four main changes to the State Department are:

A.) Eradicate unnecessary aid;

B.) Set up a system of weaning countries off of American aid through the newly-crafted United States International Development and Sustainability Agency (formerly USAID)

C.) Administer a plan for marking the American brand on the international marketplace under the newly defined Commerce Agency

D.) Take steps to ensure that we are doing

what's best for America Foreign Aid, Policy, and Commerce

6. Labor: The five main ways that the Labor Department will change are:

    A.) Include the Department of Education to focus on preparing the children to become a part of the workforce

    B.) Eliminate all unions. The National Labor Relations Board will be eradicated;

    C.) The Equal Employment Opportunity Commission will remove quotas based on race, ethnicity and any other arbitrary factor. Instead, companies will be encouraged and free to hire the most qualified applicants

    D.) The Federal Labor Relations Authority will have duties similar to the Office of Personnel Management. They will recruit, hire, train, and fire government employees

    E.) The National Mediation Board is an agency that has now become obsolete because the railway is now federalized. Their responsibilities of oversight of the railroad disputes will be taken over by the Federal Labor Relations Authority

7. Homeland: Three essential changes to the Department of Homeland Security:

    A.) Reel in the powers of the PATRIOT Act

    B.) Take on the responsibilities of the Department of Transportation to ensure collaboration between the Department of Energy and protection from disgruntled foreign interests

C.) Levy stiff penalties and jail time to individuals who hire illegal immigrants. Allow for a gateway to citizenship for current people from foreign nations who are living in the United States illegally

With these seven departments, the currently existing departments will be consolidated to simply things within our government and to greatly improve efficiency.

Part Three will focus on two new departments that also include old governmental agencies. However, these departments will ensure that the United States federal government is brought to the 21st century and this government continues to stay there through perpetual review of what's working and what's not working in various departments and agencies across the federal government.

PART THREE:

New Executive Departments

Introduction

By exploring the responsibilities and scopes of the existing Executive Departments, I dedicated my analysis in Part Two to the consolidation and elimination of several departments. In Part Three, I turn my attention to the two new departments that I will form. These new departments will reflect what Taft had hoped for the executive department in 1913: a consolidation and reorganization of the federal government based on the contemporary needs of the country. Like Taft, I believe that nine departments are enough and that "no new department ought to be created without a reorganization of all departments in the government and a redistribution of the bureaus between them."[lxxi] As I progress in my Kingdom, I may end up making that a constitutional amendment.

Two new departments will be added to the Executive Branch of the United States of America. The first will be explored in Chapter Ten and it is called the Community Development & Sustainability (CDS) Department. The CDS will oversee the redistribution of tasks from the federal government to the communities of the United States. Essentially, this new department will assist local governments with the programs that have been transferred from the jurisdiction of the federal government to the responsibility of the state and local governments. Oversight of agencies like Agriculture and the Food and Drug Administration will develop methods for ensuring that local farms and pharmaceutical companies will be practicing ethical, sustainable methods for serving their individual communities. A community commerce department paired with the local-centric Health and Human Services and the Housing and Urban Development agencies will promote enhancement of state-based approaches to empowering individuals. Also in the CDS, the Interior and the National Capital Planning Commission will enhance the outdoor and indoor federal spaces that need upkeep and maintenance. This new department is the safety net for local communities. It will ensure local constituents are aided in the best possible way.

Chapter Eleven will describe the Department of Consolidation, Coordination, & Ethics (DOC), which I will establish to ensure that my administration's changes to the federal government remain in place. The Department of Consolidation, Coordination, & Ethics (DOC) will be the prescription for failing federal plans, systems, agencies and departments. One of those systems will be centralized with the newly established Office of Science and Technology, which will ensure the consolidation of the technological systems and websites of the various federal departments. In order to ensure a total centralization-process, several agencies will be folded into the Office of Science and Technology. These agencies include the Federal Election Commission (FEC), the Federal Communications Commission (FCC), the General Services Administration (GSA), the National Security Administration (NSA), and the National Archives and Records Administration (NARA). The DOC will also take on the powers of a number of agencies which will include the Merit Protection Board, the Office of Government Ethics, the Broadcasting Board of Governors, the National Science Foundation, the Transportation Board, and the Environmental Protection Agency. The DOC will ensure that ineffective programs are efficiently identified in order to focus on their revitalization, revamping, or elimination.

Through the implementation of these last two departments, I will be completing my analysis of the federal government and the things that need to be done to ensure that we continue to prosper and thrive as a country.

Chart 18: New Executive Departments

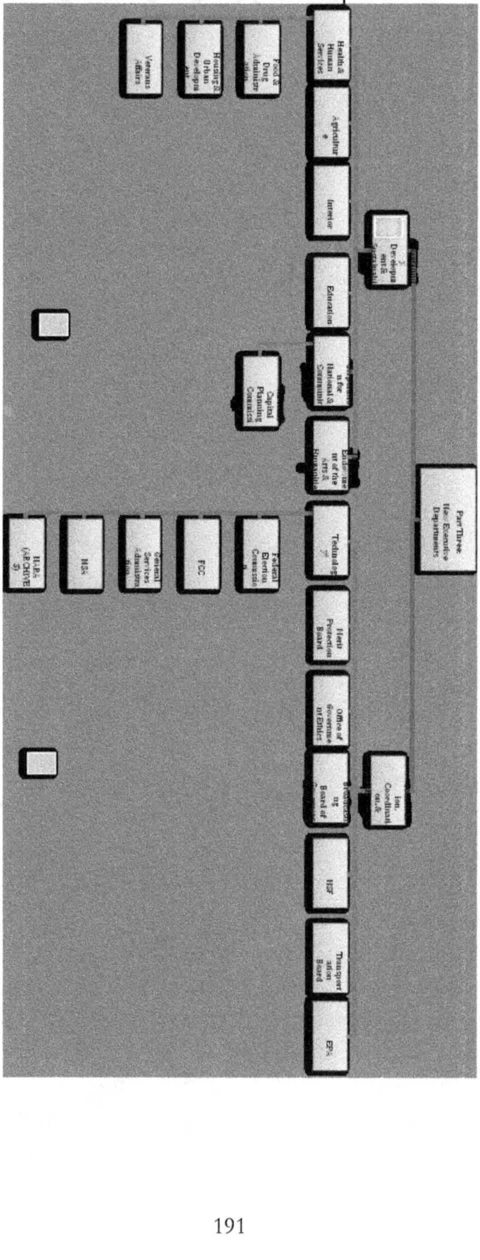

Ten:
Department of Community Development & Sustainability

I. Mission Statement: Act as a Liaison between the federal government and local communities in a coordinated effort to help local leaders access federal funding and obtain resources within the federal government in order to implement and sustain successful ideas for community improvement.

II. Agencies
    A.) Agriculture
    B.) Community Commerce Department
    C.) Food and Drug Administration
    D.) Interior
    E.) Health & Human Services
    F.) Housing and Urban Development
    G.) National Capital Planning Commission
    H.) Veterans Affairs

III. Royal Secretary: Malone Mitchell, III

Introduction

The Department of Community Development and Sustainability (CDS) will incorporate several departments and agencies that are addressing the needs of the local community. Once leaders determine the needs of their local community they will then gain access federal block grants to fund these new agencies. The Department of Community Development and Sustainability will swallow up the responsibilities of four departments: Agriculture, Health & Human Services, Interior, and Veterans Affairs. Further, they will also take on the responsibilities of the

National Capital Planning Commission, Food and Drug Administration, and Housing and Urban Development.

Under my new structure, the federal government's general mission will be to promote a workforce that is the best in the world, by bringing our federal government technologically ahead of other countries, by feeding our people, by having a healthy lifestyle, and by protecting America from global thermal nuclear war. The CDS will carry out that mission statement by coordinating with local towns and states. This coordination will include block grants that are earned through performance and brainstorming with local leaders to select and bring to bear community programs that will most work for their particular location.

Under my Kingdom, we will abolish welfare as we know it and we will give that burden back to the states. We will abolish unemployment insurance as we know it and give this money to the states out of our eighty percent (80%) budget for community development. Local areas will be responsible for developing their own communities that work for that region. Local leaders from the mayors' offices, Chambers of Commerce, business and their citizens will manage administration of these services to states and local communities. In order to assist with this process, the CDS will act as the liaison between the local agencies and the different federal departments.

The CDS will help states go through the bureaucracies of the federal government. The federal government isn't working fast enough or it isn't working across agencies in an efficient manner right now. It's always in a FEMA-like crisis mode. With the CDS, local communities and the federal government can be proactive rather than reactive.

Over the next couple pages, I will focus on each agency and department that has been folded into the CDS to show how this department will work along with the local communities. This department will help to create a highly educated, energy independent, smaller federal government.

My royal secretary appointment for the Department of Community Development and Sustainability (CDS) will be Malone Mitchell III. His background as a self-made oil magnate from Oklahoma, venture capitalist, agricultural leader, and philanthropist give him the necessary background to address the multiple moving parts that will be folded into the CDS. He is known for efficiency, coordination, and staying on budget. He grew Riata Energy from a $500 loan into one of the nation's largest private drillers. Mitchell sold his stake for hundreds of millions of dollars. His work in agriculture and energy will serve as an appropriate foundation for working in this department. Mitchell knows how to build, how to buy and, perhaps most importantly, how to grow companies by making use of full integration. With this experience and entrepreneurial spirit, he is well equipped to establish the new Department of Community Development and Sustainability and to come up with a feasible plan to incorporate all of these agencies under one department.

Interior & Capital Planning

The Department of the Interior will be combined with the National Capital Planning Commission to become an agency of the Community Development and Sustainability Department. It will coordinate with the Department of Energy's Pickens Plan to complement the Interior Agency's mission, which is "to protect America's natural resources and heritage, to honor our cultures and tribal communities, and to supply the energy to power our future." Much of the mission for planning and interior will focus on the development and planning of natural parks, urban centers, and resources.

While the Interior has been essential for the protection and management of the tribal reservations, my new government will make Native Americans part of the purview of the State Department. Should they want to truly be sovereign nations, then our policy for financial support should be the same for them as we have for every other nation in the world. Each Native American tribe that wants representation will have to establish embassies and they will have to be treated similarly to how America interacts with foreign nations. It's time to allow them the freedom that they have wanted, and we should move on. My ancestors committed multiple wrong against them. I wouldn't have done that, but it's now time to move on because I'm not going to be penalized indefinitely for the sins/wrongs of my forefathers.

In many ways, the Community Development and Sustainability Department will embody what the Department of the Interior should be: the department is responsible for the enhancement of the community by helping communities become sustainable and independent from the handouts of the federal government.

National Community Commerce

The Department of Commerce will be folded into the Community Development and Sustainability Department and its focus will be a state-centered commerce. The current mission statement of the Department of Commerce is to promote "job creation, economic growth, sustainable development and improved standards of living for all Americans by working in partnership with businesses, universities, communities and our nation's workers. The department touches the daily lives of the American people in many ways, with a wide range of responsibilities in the areas of trade, economic development, technology, entrepreneurship and business development, environmental stewardship, and statistical research and analysis." Under my rule, creating jobs and improving standards of living will no longer be the responsibility of the Department of Commerce. It will fall under the Health and Human Services Agency that is now a part of the Community Development and Sustainability Department.

The new Commerce Agency will foster economic growth by working with small business administration and other agencies to help technology transfer from our universities into products and services that corporate America can use. The charge of the Commerce Agency will be to help communities to interact with one another in trade.

Under my reign, this department will also be responsible for consumer protection. The Commerce Agency should be the watchdog of commerce and it should protect consumers from each other. An example of this happens when a company is selling corn at a loss in order to put a neighboring farmer out of business. The Commerce Agency will be responsible for calling this company out for such unfair trade practices.

Housing and Urban Development (HUD)

Very quickly, HUD will become part of the CDS, and it will make a plan to be privatized over the next couple years. HUD's mission is to create strong, sustainable, inclusive communities and quality affordable homes for all. HUD is working to strengthen the housing market to bolster the economy and to protect consumers. Through the work of HUD, and subsequently the CDS, we will continue to point our efforts toward meeting the need for quality affordable rental homes utilizing housing as a platform for improving the quality of life, and building inclusive and sustainable communities free from discrimination.

Sustainable, Community Agriculture

Agriculture
  1.)   2011: 21.7 billion
  2.)   2012: 23.9 billion

Prior to the infestation that destroyed the singular root vegetable crop of Ireland; the potato had already been on the decline. The Irish farmer needed to eat ever larger portions of potatoes to sustain their daily caloric needs. When the potato crop was decimated because of an insect infestation, the Irish had no other crop to turn to that could sustain their nutritional needs or economical needs. As a result, the Potato Famine led to one of the worst crop blights in Modern Western History. Almost a century later, a similar plight occurred on our American soil when a drought led to the "Dust Bowl" which greatly contributed to the decimation of the American economy during the 1930s. We cannot plan for natural disasters, but we can put together good plans for how to deal with them when they come. Both Ireland and 1930s America failed to do this.

Today, the problem with agriculture in the United States stems from the issues related to genetically modified crops. Genetic alteration of crops has become big business, which has led to corporations using competitive practices that, to put it as mildly as possible, are less than ideal. You can bet that the royal scepter will come down hard on those corporations.

We also need to be looking ahead with the modifications we make. Regular corn has a root system of six to seven inches deep. Genetically modified corn is about half that number. You'd think this would be beneficial until you realize that root systems create more dirt. Without a deep root system, crops are not regenerating the soil to create enough dirt. While this is not a problem today, years down the road we will be entering another possible potato famine or Dust Bowl. What can we do to avert that kind of disaster? We can take closer looks at companies who are practicing genetically modified crop development. These companies need to come up with ways to deepen the roots and nourish the soil to cultivate more dirt without losing the subtle conveniences of genetically modified farming like producing enough food to feed an ever-growing population.

Another problem with how we approach agriculture is the use of unethical practices by companies trying to protect their intellectual property. I was reminded of this problem recently when I went to Amish country. While taking a hot air balloon ride over the fields of corn in Pennsylvania, I developed a concern for the future of Amish farmers when thinking about the tactics used by Monsanto. Monsanto, one of the largest and wealthiest seed companies in the world, has been defending its empire using, in my opinion, unethical competitive practices. They have sued over 150 farmers for using their genetically modified corn without permission.

How did these 150 farmers get the corn? Monsanto is claiming they stole the corn without permission. However, the details of this alleged "theft" show a different story. Farmers did not physically take the seeds and plant them in their fields. The pollen from neighboring Monsanto farms had blown into the fields of the smaller farmers. Some of these farms are owned by people who grow organic crops and other farms are run by Amish who produce their own seeds. Monsanto is claiming patent infringement from the farms that are using the crops that grow from this accidental fertilization. The multinational company has filed suit against the small farmers for using their seed without permission.[lxxii] How does Monsanto know about the corn? They have essentially spied on local farmers and have sued the farmers found to have had Monsanto's patented gene in the farmers' plants from cross pollination. This is done, of course, in the interest of eliminating a competitor. If there is a criminal here, what honest person could argue that it is the rural farmers and not Monsanto?

In my view, Monsanto is in fact trespassing on these farmers' lands, polluting their crops with non-organic pollen. Fortunately, some farmers have seen it this way. 300,000 farmers have formed an alliance and they are suing Monsanto.[lxxiii] The case was dismissed by a judge in early 2012, but the plaintiffs have appealed the judge's decision.[lxxiv]

I believe, at the very least, Monsanto's tactics are frivolous. Monsanto shouldn't be permitted to claim the cross pollinated plants as infringing its patents if plants grown from Monsanto's seeds let the pollen loose. If that happens, I believe that the pollen becomes public domain. If anyone has a right to sue, it is the farmers. They should sue Monsanto for not containing their pollen and for trespassing. Trespassing is actually a criminal offense and should presently be handled by the Attorney General. In the Monsanto Case, the constant uncontrolled spread of Monsanto's pollen should void their patent and become public domain.

Finally, food subsidies are a costly venture in the United States. In 2011, the total cost of food subsidies was 15.2 billion dollars.[lxxv] In chart 14, I have included the top ten subsides for each year from 2003 through 2011. Corn farms have been the number one recipients of subsidies. Disaster, Cotton, Soybean and Wheat have consistently remained among the top recipients of U.S. farm subsidies. Other agricultural products appear in the top ten are Rice, Peanuts, Sorghum, Livestock, Tobacco, and Barley. In addition to Disaster Relief, three programs have appeared in the top ten subsidies: Conservation Reservation, Dairy, and Environmental Quality Inc. Programs. There are millions of companies and small farms that receive subsidies from the United States government.

This government dole of farms has to stop. The communities throughout the United States need to come up with individualized plans that allow them to grow products in a profitable, sustainable method. This method cannot include getting funding from the U.S. government. How can they become more sustainable? By using as much space as possible to grow and develop gardens and small farms. This could include rooftop farming. For example, Curt Collier has an innovative program in New York called Groundworks, NYC. He has shown that growing crops on all of the rooftops in the city would actually produce enough food to feed a large city. In addition to creating jobs in the city, using local farming methods like rooftop gardens could sustain 85% of all vegetables consumed in NYC for an entire year. The trick is to convince the Donald Trumps of the world to let people grow vegetables on their roofs.

The argument is simple: this type of rooftop farming does a lot of great things for the buildings and communities. Rooftop farming allows a city's structures to be more energy efficient since they absorb the rain waters into the gardens. Additionally, people can work together using the time banking methods that will be discussed in Health and Human services. We can start by making large cities like New York more sustainable, and work our way to smaller cities and towns.

The key problems considered by this new department include:

1.) Establishing a wider distribution of farms throughout the United States through the use of Community Farming Associations

2.) Extinguishing farm, seed, and crop monopolies

3.) Eliminating the manufacturing and distribution of unhealthy foods

4.) Constructing and implementing a plan to terminate federal food subsidies over the next five years.

Mitchell Malone could work with Dr. John E. Ikerd to figure out ways to spread our American farms around the country rather than have them concentrated in one area. Dr. Ikerd has over 30 years of experience working in the fields of Agriculture and Economics. He has worked on sustainable agriculture with a variety of organizations and agencies including the USDA, the Department of Energy, the EPA, and the Missouri Department of Natural Resources and Agriculture. Having worked on the state and local levels, he will be well-equipped to advise Malone about how to apply federal block grants to local agricultural projects. Although we will touch upon the consumption of unhealthy foods, the second point will be most fully addressed by the community supported agriculture centers.

Part of the mission statement of the Community Development and Sustainability focuses on agriculture. The CDS will provide leadership in applying and maintaining sustainable community food projects, agriculture, natural resources, and related issues based on sound public policy, the best available science, and efficient management. In essence, the country will eradicate monoculture, or the focus on producing one crop in a certain area rather than a multitude of crops. Our example in Ireland is relevant to this contention. The Irish were so blighted during the 19th century potato famine because they had no auxiliary crop. As the Irish learned, being too reliant on one crop is ludicrously risky. Farmers need to ensure diversification of our crops to protect this country from economic collapse. The agricultural goal of my Community Development and Sustainability Department is to help local cities and states build and rebuild sustainable community supported agriculture to create further diversification and move away from the devastation of monoculture. The happy side effect of crop diversity is more local jobs.

Subsidy (in millions)	2007	2008	2009	2010	2011
Corn	3805.91	4194.19	3788.18	3517.92	4610.46
Cotton	2541.48	/	2217.01	/	1297.59
Conserv. Res. Prog.	1954.86	1899.24	1865.36	1818.03	1826.66
Wheat	1618.34	2045.69	2131.99	1743.79	2023.95
Soybean	1183.62	2048.18	1675.33	1561.16	2073.45
Disaster	/	2063.64	/	2532.62	/

Chart 19: Top ten subsidies, 2003-2011.[lxxvi]

Health and Human Services Agency

Health & Human Services & Housing and Urban Development

In the 1980s Edward Cahn set in motion events leading to the development of a community-building system nationwide. Dr. Cahn thought about ways people could receive what they want or need in exchange for committing time or their skills in exchange for someone else's time or skills. For example, one uninsured man might give an elderly man a ride to the doctor in exchange for access to health care services. Dr. Cahn's system has been an effective way to allow people to receive something useful or fun in exchange for helping their neighbors.

In a September 2010 *New York Times* Article, entitled *"Where All Work Is Created Equal,"* Tina Rosenberg describes how these time banks have evolved where "the unit of currency is not a dollar, but an hour," so that "A 90-year-old can contribute on an equal basis with a 30 year old." People could participate without worry of being taxed for the time, as the Internal Revenue Service's has determined hours not to be taxable. In Japan, *Fureai Kipu* (or Caring Relationships) is a type of time banking where helping the elderly will allow the participants to save up time that could be used when they have reached the point when they will need companions to assist or accompany them on shopping trips and doctor's visits.

***

To help with developing the new CDS, Malone Mitchell will develop more efficient and effective community-based welfare and health programs. In 2012, the budget for Health and Human Services was 79.9 billion dollars; the Housing and Urban Development was budgeted for 48 billion; and the Veterans Affairs had a budget of 61.85 billion dollars.

The Health and Human Services Department has expanded and contracted over the decades since it was formally established in 1953 under President Eisenhower. Initially it was called the Department of Health, Education and Welfare and it became its own entity in 1979. On May 4, 1980, HEW became the Department of Health and Human Services. Under my reign, Health and Human Services will become an agency with the mission to help provide the building blocks that American children, families, veterans, and seniors need to live healthy, successful lives by reinvesting into community supported programs such as healthcare, food safety, and disease prevention.

The new Health and Human Resources Agency will work to abolish welfare as it currently exists across the country. Americans would implement this system to "help provide the building blocks Americans need to live healthy, successful lives." Malone Mitchell could work with Ed Cahn of TimeBank America and Dr. Edward Miller of Johns Hopkins to revamp the Health and Human Resources Agency. They are both highly qualified to assist Malone Mitchell with the problems related to welfare. Ed Cahn would lead a team to develop ways to tackle the real problems of the welfare system, while Ed Miller will develop a public health care system that works.

Welfare: Empower Not Enable the People

Ronald Regan said that the best way is not reform, rather the best way to address welfare is to abolish it entirely. I agree. We have to bring health care back to the local community. Our American communities need to work as a unit to educate, employ, feed, clothe, and all around empower our people. Each community has its own issues and the issues relevant to the poor in Charleston are different from those who need assistance in Chicago. Each community needs to take care of the problem based on the needs of the people who live in a particular location. Ironically, the biggest impediment to welfare working at present is that the welfare system is federalized, and is therefore incapable of coexisting with the nuance of local needs.

Under our new system, the federal government will give out block grants to communities who come up with effective and efficient ways to address the issues of feeding and employing its people in need. The goal is to teach them to fish not to give them money to buy a fish. Cahn could train Health and Human Services representatives to travel around the country to train community members in time-banking. Whether a religious or non-profit organization, if they come up with a way to increase the employability and decrease or eradicate the need for welfare as it currently stands, the organization/community will be able to lobby for this money. In addition to time banking, they might develop soup kitchens, job fairs, and more.

Welfare will not be eradicated overnight, and my task force would come up with a multi-year plan to ensure that everyone in every town forms a community. This will move us one step closer to being a strong, healthier, and happier United States. Americans tend to be very generous with their charitable donations. We are probably one of the most giving nations in the history of the world. We can retain this generosity, this giving nature, by giving strength and autonomy to our people.

The crime in the welfare system is that we are paying people not to work. While hard working Americans earn their income, the welfare collectors are sitting around and watching television; they are collecting their food stamps to eat unhealthy foods. We need to abolish welfare altogether. We will use less money by directly funding the communities to help their people. One way to press for change is to create a federal challenge to the community that does the best. The community that does the best will have the most productive people.

Basically, federal funding for health and human services programs will be based on a productivity matrix. The more productive the people in a community, the lower the crime rate. Productivity has also been shown to increase one's sense of self-worth, suggesting that more productive communities will be happier. Immigrants will be treated more fairly, with the criminalization of hiring illegal immigrants falling on the shoulders of the employers. However, they should be paid a fair wage but they should not be able to access welfare programs.

By allowing welfare to fester in its current form, the recipients have become disenfranchised from participation in our opportunistic society. Without being involved in the community, people in need will feel more and more entitled, and that entitlement flows down to their children creating generations of welfare recipients. If we don't do something about this culture of entitlement, the loss of work ethic and the devastation of the entrepreneurial spirit will lead to all manner of societal woes like higher crime rates. By changing the way things are done, these recipients will become productive members of a community with a stake in what happens in that community. For example, individuals will be rewarded for giving some time to help out an elderly neighbor.

Finally, illegal immigrants will no longer be eligible to receive any welfare. As King, I will ensure that immigrants will be treated more fairly, with the criminalization of hiring illegal immigrants falling on the shoulders of the employers. However, they should not be getting as much as Americans who are citizens and they should not be able to access welfare until they have become official citizens of the country. In 2009, fifty-two percent (52%) of households with children headed by legal immigrants were on at least one welfare program. Seventy-one percent (71%) of illegal immigrants with children were enrolled in a welfare program. These people deserve a fair chance, but at the end of the day they are here illegally. We should work on getting them to become citizens so they can participate in the give and take nature of the American community. We should not be rewarding them with the fiscal benevolence of human services if they're unwilling to become part of America in any way but their location. The fact that they have children who are legal residents does not take away from the fact that they are defrauding the federal government. This needs to stop. We need to reward the people who do the right thing, and expel those who do not. We will offer them avenues to being in the U.S. legally (visa, residency, and citizenship) and, if they do not want to play by the fair rules of our country, then they must leave the country immediately.

Another example of the welfare system gone wrong: people having children to further milk the system. Single women continue to have children to obtain an increase in their income. We are literally paying people to have more of what they cannot afford. People are having more kids just to get more money every month from the federal government. It's just the wrong incentive to give to people who are already needy, who have low self-worth, and who do not have skills to enter the job market. It just isn't fair for a single non-working mother to be making more on welfare than a single mother who is employed as a school teacher.

The solution to this problem is to empower the women and men who seek state assistance. Make these individuals feel comfortable and confident in themselves by preparing them through education and training rather than neglecting those qualities through a financial transfusion. There are people who will never be able to fend for themselves, and they need protection from their local communities. Individuals who need particular care are the indigent, the mentally challenged, and the wards of the state. A jobless mother with seven children does not necessarily fall into one of these categories. So, in order to empower her, she could run the local community daycare center including her seven children.

Individual communities will have a good idea for addressing the needs of their people. Usually, these ideas would work but they may not have the funding to build the infrastructure. In such cases, they will be able to appeal to the Department of Community Development and Sustainability for block grants and these block grants can be used to build the necessary infrastructure. In order to receive money, they will have to establish, to a very high standard of doubt, that they will not need the money again. They will have to have a plan in-hand to sustain their new programs without multi-year financial doles from the federal government.

Success can come in many forms. For example, in education a school system will have to demonstrate the value they are going to get for the funding that they receive. Are their students graduating? Getting jobs? Are they helping the homeless find work? The grant application has a burden of proof to show the Department of Community Development and Sustainability that the money they receive will produce a positive outcome for their greater community.

Although there should be separation of Church and State, we won't be concerned about religion as long as they are coming up with good ideas for supplying for the needy citizens of their community. In order to ensure that there is not an overwhelming turn to religion, only twenty percent (20%) of all community block grants can be used by religious organizations. The decision-makers will not consider religion a major factor in distributing these grants. If a Christian Church wants to open up a soup kitchen or a Muslim mosque wants to host a job fair, they are not exempt from accessing this money. This doesn't mean they can get a grant to give out bibles and hold religious events. It does mean they can lead by example providing non religious services to their community. The community needs to work together and come up with viable solutions to the problem. That's the goal. The citizens of the United States have become detached from their communities, and it lies at the heart of a lot of our problems. We have to replace the idea of take, take, take with the concepts of giving back to the community, of doing what's best for the country, and so on.

An additional incentive for empowering local constituents will come from Congressmen and Senators. One of the Royal Amendments states that Congressional pay will be based on the average income for their district. By giving Congress the possibility of a pay raise, they will have a personal stake in ensuring the income of their constituents also increases. While there will always be people who are below the poverty line, the community will be motivated to do the right thing. With all of these community programs, more people will be working. With the current system of welfare, those people already don't count. They've been disenfranchised from the mainstream system. Since they bring down your average income, you now have a personal stake in getting them off of welfare and getting them to work. This new system will bring up that number by introducing accountability to the people at the top.

During the Civil War, the Great Depression, and 9/11, citizens of the U.S. have come together as a nation; they have strengthened the bonds of the community. We should not need travesties to form communities. Tightly-woven communities are the strength of humanity, not just the United States. We can be one of the most giving nations in world. That part of our national psyche will never let us down.

Social Security

At the onset of reeling in social security, the program's taxation on businesses will be eliminated. Because I am eliminating the Social Security tax imposed on businesses, companies can use that extra funding to reinvest into the company, hire more people, and do a lot of other wonderful things for the Americans in their employ. The local communities will receive a percentage of the surplus money because of the people who did not accept their Social Security payoff. Whichever region they come from will receive a portion of the payoff that the individual refused. Incidentally, this will be another way to get a block grant for the community. The individual giving their portion of Social Security to the community will work alongside local governments to decide how to handle and help their people.

If individuals are over the age of 75, and their net worth is less than two million dollars, they will be exempt from the national consumption tax on any single purchase under $500. It's important to get the hands of the governments off of it. Social Security will serve the country in a more powerful manner when it is eradicated and it is used as block grants to support community-driven programs for the needy. The people who have already contributed to Social Security should be able to access the money that they put into their funds.

Access to Health Care

There are two services that every American needs: education and healthcare. Education will be given to the states, but healthcare is a different story. Ron Paul has been promoting essential changes to the healthcare system that make sense. One of his more delightful quotes is that it's bad to be uninsured and it's worse to be insured. Neither method is working. We need to find something that's at least better than bad.

Under my Kingdom, five major changes will be put into effect for the health care system:

1.) Block grants will be given to counties based on individual needs
2.) Healthcare professionals must disclose all business interests
3.) State borders will be open to insurance companies
4.) Creation of incentives for preventive health methods
5.) Individuals will not be required to have healthcare and businesses will not be required to offer these kinds of benefits. This would mean the demise of the Patient Protection and Affordable Care Act

Healthcare will be a community issue. People who are on the poverty level will have access to community block grant programs for healthcare. In order to receive these grants, county governments must come up with viable, sustainable solutions to ensuring their people have access to healthcare. This should be individualized because people from Frederick, Maryland will have different needs than people from Anchorage, Alaska.

Further, all subsidies given to hospitals must be disclosed. Doctors need to nullify their conflicts of interest with insurance companies, labs, health supply vendors and pharmaceutical companies. As such, they should also be made to disclose any investments that are related to these vendors and pharmaceutical companies. In particular, investments that are not publically traded companies. Publically traded companies will not be impacted as much if one or two patients are referred to the products. However, doctors will be prohibited from investing in any businesses that are conflicts of interest. For example, should a surgeon have a use for a lab test, that surgeon needs to avoid investing in or owning that lab. By putting this rule in place, this will prevent surgeons from encouraging patients to do unnecessary procedures in order to fatten their pockets.

With regards to access to insurance companies, this is where the federal government needs to be in control, which means that some states will lose rights. As it currently stands, insurance companies need to be "accredited" to offer insurance in each state. Some states have allowed for the development of mini-monopolies which are an enormous detriment to keeping healthcare affordable. This has created a non-capitalistic, non-competitive market. Finally, each state has a list of what can and cannot be covered. This is causing a bottleneck of service and coverage. Consumers who are paying for their insurance are not allowed access to the service for which they are paying.

Under my Kingdom, the country will be every insurance company's oyster. As mentioned in Chapter Four, should insurance companies want to practice in more than a couple states, they will now be subject to Section 18 of the National Securities Market Improvement Act of

1996. This will reduce expenses by not having so much overlap in every state. Lawyers will only have to research the federal mandates instead of each mandate of each state in which the insurance company offers coverage. Further, the offices could consolidate by region. By consolidating and creating competition, prices will become more competitive. An additional benefit to Americans is that they will now have loads more options. Consumers will be able to go to another company if one company is overcharging for their services. This will put an end to the bureaucratic rules that each state has for what can and cannot be provided and covered.

Because insurance will now be specialized (typical ailments in South Carolina will differ from those in Illinois), a company may decide to practice in only one state, several states or all states. If a company offers service nationally, they don't have to follow the blue sky laws in each of the states. These companies only have to adhere to the national standards. If they are a small insurance company that only wants to practice in Texas, then they can still do that under the same rules as the big guys' offerings everywhere. This added competition will only help with insurance costs. Having health insurance companies follow the same guidelines as companies that are listed on the public exchanges makes a lot of sense.

Another element of healthcare that will be changed is our approach to treatment. We will focus on preventive rather than reactive healthcare. Agencies like the FDA will promote healthy living not by taking a pill or by waiting until there is a catastrophe, but by providing incentives that get people to live in a fashion that reduces pills and catastrophes. Health insurance has to include a visit to the doctor once a month. For problems like obesity, food manufacturers will be required to offer food in appropriate portion sizes. Further, educating people about appropriate eating habits must be a priority. People who choose the right habits will be granted a reprieve because packaged and frozen foods are taxed, while flour and cheese are untaxed. Basically, if you make your own pizza rather than buy it frozen or from a restaurant, you will not pay the tax.

The school systems will be involved with collaborating local businesses to promote healthy eating habits. The schools will have to work with community supported agriculture centers. Even in concrete Metropolis of New York City the schools can create rooftop gardens. Perhaps have the local McDonalds sponsor athletics for high schools. Since athletics will become privatized, this could be a prime way of continuing athletics in the public school system. This sponsorship would be a way to have corporate dollars paying for something that's good for the society and local community. This will be a win-win for McDonalds and the athletics department. The fast-food chain will be branding their name and the students will be able to have access to a high quality athletics department. This sponsorship will pay for something that the county might have had to pay for otherwise, thereby saving the federal government and local community a substantial amount of dollars. This encouragement of investment into the community from local, albeit international, business will only strengthen the community.

As for healthcare included in benefits packages, the requirements should remain the same. That is, in a free market, businesses shouldn't be required to offer its employees health care. Of course, they can choose to provide healthcare in order to be viable contenders for employing the best workers. The emancipation of businesses from restrictions means we should strive to bring the problems of the community back to community members. Of course, with a competitive healthcare market, employers may be inclined to offer one hundred percent (100%) health insurance because the costs are so low. Frankly, employees are still going to demand raises and other benefits. Since employers are not paying income tax as a business any longer, and because CEOs will no longer be able to pocket exorbitant sums, they may be more inclined to give that money to employees through benefits like health care.

Now might be an appropriate time to remind readers that federal officials will no longer have access to super health care systems, fantastic benefits for life, and awesome retirement packages. This will give our leaders a new incentive to make sure our needs are taken care of first, since their benefits depend on ours. Lifetime salaries for two years of service are over. As we stated, the only way a congressman could get a pay raise is to increase the pay of people in his or her district. Further, they will have the same housing allowance that we grant to the military, based on location. This will be adjusted based on the location. For example, people in Sedona Arizona will have a different cost of living than people from New York City. As for health insurance, government officials will all have access to the same health insurance that is offered to the military. Our officials are now part of our communities. They thrive or suffer with the rest of us.

Food & Drug Administration

Another agency that will be folded into the Department of Community Development and Sustainability is the Food and Drug Administration. The current FDA mission is to protect "the public health by assuring the safety, efficacy and security of human and veterinary drugs, biological products, medical devices, our nation's food supply, cosmetics, and products that emit radiation." The FDA will be required to have full transparency. This transparency will show up by informing the consumer of all contents in the food they eat. If they are sold in stores and if a person can ingest it, the FDA is responsible for ensuring that Americans are informed about what they are ingesting. If any company wants to sell to Americans, they will have to explain all that is inside.

Another current responsibility of the FDA is to ensure food security and to foster development of safe medical products. The FDA will work with the Agriculture agency to create and support a nationwide development of community-supported agricultural programs. Further, the FDA will be involved in determining distribution of food subsidies. We are going to ensure that these subsidies are cut in half if not eliminated entirely.

***

Welfare, Agriculture, and Food and Drug Administration will work together under the Department of Community Development and Sustainability. The responsibility for Agriculture will ensure that communities receive grants to develop dedicated pieces of land that are big enough to feed their particular communities. These fields will be community-supported agricultural centers that grow no less than fifty percent (50%) of the food consumed by the region. These centers will not be permitted to be monoculture systems. They must grow a variety of foods for their communities. As a result, food costs will decrease because there will be a decrease in the market for vegetables and other produce shipped from all over the world. The lower costs of transportation and food storage will contribute to the decrease in food prices. By working with the Agriculture agency to ensure the development of locally based agriculture centers, the FDA will ensure that there will be less of a chance of total annihilation during disasters.

Crops will no longer be genetically modified, and people will be motivated to eat healthier food option.

By eliminating all subsidies, the money will now be available to be recycled back into the community where is can be used to train/educate locals and help them to develop the skills they need to be gainfully employed in that region. This means that a part of the secondary education system will be focused on teaching students about agriculture for the local community. Because we will no longer be contributing to these mega-corporations, there will be a development of hundreds of thousands of jobs in agriculture nationwide resulting in less of a need for genetically-modified crops. Our federal legislature will work with the Department of Community Sustainability and Development to ensure the protection of our people, their jobs, their food supply, and their local farms. With these programs, the federal government will take the money out of the crimes in welfare, food production, food consumption, and education.

Conclusion

The essential elements of the Community Development and Sustainability Department relate to bridging the local communities to federal resources and general ideas related to agriculture, health and human services, food, veteran's affairs, housing, and local commerce.

With all of the departments established, we have one more watchdog task force department to discuss. I will create a new agency to ensure that the federal government remains on task. This agency will be an anti-waste, efficiency-promoting, and deregulating anti-corruption agency. One final department will be responsible for eliminating all crimes in the federal government. The Department of Consolidation, Coordination, and Ethics (DOC) will find the money in the crime, take the money out of the crime, and the crime will go away.

Eleven:
Department of Consolidation, Coordination, & Ethics

I. Mission Statement: The mission of the Department of Consolidation, Coordination, and Ethics is to serve as the official government entity that performs checks and balances to constantly monitor all departments and related agencies of the federal government. The department is responsible for overseeing how all entities of the federal government are operating and to report with suggested operational changes, eliminations, or additions. They are additionally charged with reporting these findings back to the president.

II. Agencies
   1.) Merit Protection Board
   2.) Office of Government Ethics
   3.) Broadcasting Board of Governors
   4.) National Science Foundation
   5.) Transportation Board
   6.) Environmental Protection Agency
   7.) Office of Science and Technology
       A. Federal Election Commission
       B. Federal Communications Commission
       C. General Services Administration
       D. National Security Administration
       E. National Archives and Records Administration (NARA)

III. Royal Cabinet Member: Rep. David Camp

This final department will be primarily responsible for maintaining the changes I've implemented in the federal government.

The Department of Consolidation, Coordination will be responsible for independently evaluating every department and agency in the federal government. As Herbert Hoover envisioned, before we add new entities (departments, agencies, etc.) to the federal government, it is necessary to have a thorough review of all departments to ensure the elimination of wasteful and ineffective programs and to deregulate in as many sectors of government as possible. Federal program administrators need to continually prove that they are necessary or they will be consolidated into another department or agency, revamped to suit the current needs of the country, or eliminated if there is no longer a need for the service.

The DOC will be continually looking at ways for entities of the federal government to work together in order to be more efficient and to eliminate programs that aren't paying off an investment in some way. The DOC will not be responsible for creating new programs; rather the department will be responsible for working towards a continued effort at efficiency in already existing programs. DOC officials will also be responsible for monitoring federal agencies and departments to ensure that corruption is sniffed out and eliminated. There will be no room or tolerance for corruption in the country.

What is corruption? As I discussed in the first part of this book, corruption is using the government in excessive methods to advance personal wealth and status. The DOC will be the watchdog department sniffing out these crimes and eradicating the federal government of such things.

Several agencies will be folded into the Department of Consolidation, Coordination, and Ethics. The Merit Protection Board and the Office of Government Ethics will become redundant, as the responsibility of these agencies is to ensure the just actions occur in the federal government. The Environmental Protection Agency, the Broadcasting

Board of Governors, the Transportation Board, and the National Science Foundation have oversight of specific trades and industries. Finally, a new agency will be formed to address the need for oversight of technology administration. The Office of Science and Technology will include agencies that have a heavy focus on web and records-based platforms. These agencies include the Federal Election Commission (FEC), the Federal Communications Commission (FCC), the General Services Administration (GSA), the National Security Administration (NSA), the National Archives and Records Administration (NARA).

Michigan Congressman, David Camp, is my pick for the Department of Consolidation, Coordination and Ethics. Congressman Camp is the current chairman of the Ways and Means Committee. Further, he was named a member of the Joint Select Committee on Deficit Reduction. He knows how to implement federal policies to states from a national vantage point.

The Office of Science and Technology will be responsible for the standardization of all of the government's technology-related business. The National Institute of Science and Technology will be eliminated because the Office of Science and makes the office superfluous. Any platforms and computer systems will be under the jurisdiction of the Office of Science and Technology. They will be responsible for making sure that the government has a diversified, yet compatible array of systems. Some things should be standardized. Lastly, they will work with and coordinate all of the technology purchases, installation, and maintenance for all agencies and departments according to the policies of the Office of Science and Technology.

The Office of Science and Technology will be primarily responsible for providing a standardized web presence of each government entity and for ensuring full transparency of every agency. Full transparency will include posting all the documents from all the departments that are supposed to be serving the public directly. The sites of all agencies will be standardized in a very user-friendly way so that when you learn to navigate one, you will be able to navigate them all. The Office of Science and Technology will be the watchdog to ensure that these non-classified documents will promote and maintain transparency in a timely fashion.

The General Services Administration will be in charge of coordinating the purchases for all the departments and for ensuring that what is purchased works well with current technology and platforms. That will give each agency bulk buying power even if they only need one computer. It also eliminates warehouses of stuff from each agency since the GSA, which will have ownership of these things, will be able to sell or auction off outdated unused items. For example, each agency and department has furniture and office supplies. When the department no longer has a need for the supplies, those supplies will be going back to GSA. If a position is eliminated in the Labor Department, then the desk, computer, and other supplies from that individual's office will be returned to the GSA warehouse. This will stop departmental hording.

Conclusion

This book is my call to action. In Chart 20 you can quickly glance at all of the essential changes that I would make under my royal Kingdom. From my new and revamped departments to my royal amendments implementing important tax and government structural changes, our country will be greatly improved for everyone. Because this is an election year, —every reader of this book, including you, small, optimistic, American, wonderful you, has the ability to make a difference. If nothing else, I have earned my right to complain (and believe me, I will use it) because I have given you a clear picture of where change needs to happen in the federal government. I have endeavored, to the best of an ability garnered over a successful twenty year stay in business, to give you a clear picture of how this change can be put into effect. I am not just saying we need "change," I am conceiving of solutions and contributing to the pool of ideas. So, now I ask you the questions that started this whole project: what would you do to change the government? What do you see is wrong? How can you bring America back to greatness? What would the King do? What can you do to make these changes? Whether you agree or disagree with me, right now you have the insight and tools to do something about it, talk about it and make our leaders hear you.

There are many paths that you can take, and I want to help you take the path that is best for you. If you believe in some or all of what I'm saying, stand up and tell your congressmen. If you want to see the line-item veto, if you want to see all of the restructuring amendments put into effect, stand up and tell your president-elect. How can you do this? Well by being an informed voter, obviously. But definitely continue the conversation. Help educate others. Help educate *me*.

The conversation continues at my website: kinghighusa.com. On twitter I'm @KingHighUSA. However, after all this talk of modern technology, I'd be a fool if I didn't say that most readers will join the conversation at facebook.com/kinghighusa. Ask me, on your behalf, to let your congressman, your Senator and the President, know you want these changes. Speak up as time is most certainly a luxury we *do not* have.

Finally go to town-meetings, send letters to Congress, and send letters to the President. Tweet everyone you know to get involved and to read this book.

We have to take the money out of the crime, so the

crime will go away. By taking the money out of all the ineffective programs, by giving the President line item veto power, by eliminating wasteful spending, by deregulating rather than over regulating, by changing the tax code, by encouraging the entrepreneurial spirit, America will be able to return to greatness.

Chart 20: Overview of King High's Changes.

Part One: Royal Amendments	
Qualification	
One:	The President shall be given the power of the Line-Item Veto.
Two:	*Federal Officials shall not hold an elected position while running for office. *Must be governor before running for president *2 years wait prior to taking positions with conflicts of interest.
Three:	districts must be box-shape based on longitude and latitude Consistent size through state and/or county
Four:	*President & Senators have six year terms; Congressmen have four. *No more than two terms, can be non-consecutive
Five:	*President not more than six times the median salary of the country *Congressmen no more than 3.5 times median income of their districts; *No budget No pay
Budgetary	
Six:	*Sixteenth Amendment nullified; income tax eliminated *12% consumption tax implemented.
Seven:	*20% of GDP used annually to pay debt *after debt paid, 5% of GDP put into Emergency Relief Fund

Part Two: Existing Departments	
Energy *(DOE)*	*Royal Cabinet:* T. Boone Pickens *Agencies:* Nuclear Regulatory Commission; Tennessee Valley Authority. *Changes* *Pickens' plan: 1. natural gas and other forms of energy 2. develop power grid 3. incentivize individuals to use efficient types of energy; *Consolidate all energy-related agencies; *Obtain 100% of energy from American resources.
Treasury	*Royal Cabinet:* Arthur Brooks *Agencies:* SEC (Commodity Future Trading Commission); Banking (FDIC; Nat'l Community Service Admin. [former SBA]; Farm Credit Admin.; Fed. Housing Finance Board; export/import; & Nat'l Credit Union Admin); Retirement (Fed. Retirement Thrift Board; Pension Ben. Guarantee; Nat'l RR Retirement Board; Soc. Sec). *phase out all government-retirement (Social Security); *Retire the reserve; *Eliminate the Moody's/S&P credit-rating duopoly; *Ease congressional market regulation; *silver standard; *deregulate state-based insurance industries. * Inclusion of executive compensation restrictions.

Defense (DOD)	*Royal Cabinet: Lynn Tilton* *Agencies:* Defense Nuclear Facilities Safety Board *centralize all military systems; *eliminate all redundancy; *build military supplies & vehicles in America; *buy supplies & vehicles from American companies; *re-implement constitutional declarations of war.
Justice (DOJ)	*Royal Cabinet: Brigadier General Judge James Cullen* *Agencies:* Commission of Civil Rights; FTC Postal Regulatory Commission *allow communities to legalize marijuana; *eliminate the American Rule; *incorporate powers of FTC; *reel in powers of Unions; *privatize the postal service.
State	*Royal Cabinet: Brent Scowcroft* *Agencies:* Commerce (Consumer Protection Agency); US Int'l Dev't & Sustainability (USAID); InterAmerican; African; PeaceCorps; US Trade & Dev't agency [overseas private investment corp]); and US Int'l Trade Commission. *eradicate unnecessary aid; *eliminate international welfare via U.S. Int'l Dev't Agency; *build up the American brand through the Commerce Agency; *do what's best for foreign aid, policy, and commerce.

Labor	*Royal Cabinet: Jack Welch*
	Agencies: Education; Equal Employ't Opp'y Commission; FLRA; Federal Mine Safety & Health Review Commission; National Mediation Board.
	*portfolio and community-based education (Education);
	*eradicate all unions and NLRB;
	*eradicate race-based quotas; encourage skills-based hiring;
	*Labor Relations Authority served as fed. personnel dept;
	*eliminate National Mediation Board.
Homeland DOH	*Royal Cabinet: Peter Thiel*
	Agencies: Transportation; Federal Maritime Commission; Nat'l Railroad Passenger Comm; Selective Service Comm; TSA.
	*reel in powers of PATRIOT Act;
	*attend to Nat'l transportation issues; protect from foreign interests;
	*punish employers not immigrants for hiring illegal workers.

Part Three: New Executive Departments	
Community Development & Sustainability (CDS)	*Royal Cabinet: Malone Mitchell III* *Agencies:* Agriculture; Community Commerce Dept; FDA, Interior; HHS; HUD; Nat'l Capital Planning Commission; Veterans Affairs *Mission:* oversee redistribution of tasks from federal to local gov'ts. *oversee farms and pharmaceuticals; *localized development of health and human services; time banking *planning and maintenance of public spaces *ensure ethical, sustainable, community-based methods
Consolidation, Coordination, & Ethics (DOC)	*Royal Cabinet: Rep. David Camp* *Agencies:* Merit Protection Board; Off of Gov't Ethics; Broadcasting Board of Gov; NSF; Transportation; EPA; Office of Science & Technology (FEC, FCC; GSA; NSA; NARA). *Mission:* ensure implementation of my Kingdom's changes And modify failing federal programs. *technology agency to centralize federal technological systems

KING

ACKNOWLEDGEMENTS

Writing a book is not an easy endeavor. I have taken the initiative to get this job done. However, no man is an island and I couldn't have accomplished the completion of this book without thanking a few people.

I would like to thank my son, Zachariah, for giving me the idea so many years ago, and my daughter, Alizah, for keeping me on my toes. I acknowledge my editor, Melissa Kotulski, for her hard work and enthusiasm, Mind Media Group for their dedication and relentless energy and my friend Teddy for helping getting the word out.

For any individual that I may have forgotten—family member, professional partner, friend, staff (especially Christina and Maggie), and clients—thank you for your support during this process.

I'd also like to thank the royal cabinet members whom I have appointed: T. Boone Pickens (Energy); Arthur Brooks (Treasury); Lynn Tilton (Defense); Brigadier General Judge James Cullen (Justice); Brent Scowcroft (State); Jack Welch (Labor); Peter Thiel (Homeland); Malone Mitchell III (Community Development & Sustainability); and Representative David Camp (Consolidation, Coordination, & Ethics). With people who have such compelling visions for the improvement of our country, I thank them for their work as individuals and hope that their work as a team will help to bring America back to greatness.

Finally, I have to thank our fore founders for their vision, dedication and their lives. My freedom, our freedom, would not exist today without their courage. We must maintain the strength and the sacrifice for the next generation. We must never forget that we are the greatest country on earth and with that come humbleness and humility. We must recognize when we do forget in order to take immediate action to correct.

I am honored to be an American. I give this book to you as a guide. A guide to keep the drive of what our founders like Thomas Jefferson hoped our country could grow into.

ABOUT THE AUTHOR

Who is the man who would be King of America?

Kevin J. High was born into business. His grandfather owned a grocery store in Glenn Ellen, Illinois. Kevin's father owned a restaurant and a printing company in Chicago where Kevin spent a good portion of his youth keeping the floors nice and shiny. But it afforded him the opportunity to learn the ins and outs of small business.

In 1977 Kevin moved to Maryland to live with his sister and to work on her farm. Cleaning up after livestock was a humble beginning for a would-be king, but learning the value of farm life suited Kevin just fine. During that time he also worked with his sister and her husband's court-reporting company in a suburb of Washington DC. Shortly thereafter the company met with tremendous fortune when it became the official court reporter for the Carter White House.

Though he enjoyed the work on the farm, at 13 years-old politics bit Kevin and bit him deep. While going to school and keeping his job at his sister's business, he was able to be in the White House serving as a page. He was almost literally a fly on the wall during the last year of the Carter administration and for three years into Reagan's Presidency. This was a good time for Kevin, who recalls feeling a tremendous sense of awe for the political process.

After some unfortunate events with his family he immediately, after graduating high school, started his own court reporting company after a friend's father co-signed a $3000 loan to get him started. His company became one of the first companies in the state of Maryland, DC and Virginia to offer video tape depositions. At 18 years-old, Kevin was already a notary public in Maryland, DC and Virginia. As that business became successful he decided to branch out and start a restaurant in Frederick, Maryland. Unfortunately, it all came down due to location and cash flow. Turns out you don't hit a home run every time, and Kevin learned a very valuable lesson.

Starting all over again, Kevin decided that he needed to go to college. He decided on Salisbury State where he majored in business. At only 20 years-old, as a student, he started a successful advertising business which held contracts with both Kentucky Fried Chicken and the Marines. His classes, combined with this new successful business, made it clear to Kevin that investment banking was where he needed to be. In 1987, at 22, he dropped out of college and became a stock broker. Soon after, he joined Shearson Lehman Hutton (which would later become Smith Barney) and quickly became one of their top producers.

In 1990 Kevin was married, and in 1991 he moved to Rhode Island to start a family. Rhode Island was a good fit for Kevin with its proximity to the heavy business districts of Boston and New York.

In 1994 Kevin resigned from Smith Barney and founded the Corporate Securities Group in Middletown, RI. This new freedom from a big bank like Smith Barney afforded Kevin the opportunity to work with companies of all sizes, but particularly with small companies like the ones in which he had grown up. In 1997, Kevin sold that branch to the brokers he had worked with. But Kevin was nowhere near done with business. The wave of internet business was rising and Kevin was at its crest. He immediately founded and invested in a series of web-based companies, one of which was Collegelink.com. Through a series of acquisitions that site was expanded to include a company called Making It Count and was later sold to Monster.com in June of 2001.

Two months later, on September 11th, 2001, the World Trade Center was attacked. Fortunately, Kevin was not there that day. Even before that tragic day the dot com bubble had taken its toll on Kevin. The markets were all but dead and the businesses that were Kevin's life and expertise no longer existed. Being between companies, having worked for 20 years, and feeling burnt out under the weight of personal financial losses all on top of having lost so many people he knew in the 9/11 attacks, Kevin decided he needed a disconnect. It was decided that the family would take an extended sailing trip, which they did for almost three years. This was a time of reflection for Kevin, where the reverence he'd once had for the governmental process as a Washingtonian gave way to an ever-growing cynicism. Re-examining the cogs of government with a full knowledge of how finances and businesses work stripped away much of their luster.

Even on the high seas, Kevin couldn't stop his mind from returning to business. Near the end of 2002 he had discovered a company called Solomon Technology. That company conceived and produced several new innovations, including an electric motor for boats. In 2003 Kevin agreed to help the company raise capital and to take it public. Due to the new legislation making it harder for small businesses to get off the ground, it was a battle. But Kevin managed to raise the company several million dollars from the comfort of his boat as well as several trips to the Charleston Public Library, partially to work on his business and partially because he had fallen in love with the city.

In April of 2004 it was time to return to the world full-bore. Kevin's new home was Charleston where he founded Sequence Investment Partners, which included all of the maneuvering to make Sequence a registered Broker Dealer with the SEC. Again, due to collapse in the economy and other family issues, not to mention the reactionary new legislation creating new hurdles for small businesses, Sequence Investment Partners entered into an agreement with Webster Rodgers and changed its name to WRSequence. Kevin later sold his equity share in the company. He now manages his investments and works as a consultant.

Oh! And ever since 2010, he's been writing a book; this book.

When not running a business or contemplating politics, Kevin is an avid sailor and photographer. He has both a son and daughter who both make him very proud.

One of his personal heroes and his good friend Mark Bryan (of Hootie and the Blowfish fame) who grew up in the same Neighborhood as Kevin, though they did not really become friends until Kevin moved to Charleston. Kevin is very grateful to Mark for his influences on parenting in particular.

[i] <u>Thomas Jefferson</u> to William Stephens Smith, <u>Paris</u>, 13 Nov. 1787.
[ii] Brooks, Albert. *The Battle: How the Fight between Free Enterprise and Big Government Will Shape America's Future.* p 17.
[iii] *Clinton V. City of New York.* The Oyez Project at IIT Chicago-Kent College of Law. 10 January 2012.
[iv] Term Limits: The Only Way to Clean Up Congress, By <u>Dan Greenberg</u>, *August 10, 1994.* <u>http://www.heritage.org/research/reports/1994/08/bg994 nbsp-term-limitsnbsp-the-only-way</u>
[v] Term Limits: The Only Way to Clean Up Congress, By <u>Dan Greenberg</u>, *August 10, 1994.* <u>http://www.heritage.org/research/reports/1994/08/bg994 nbsp-term-limitsnbsp-the-only-way</u>
[vi] Twenty out of 43 presidents served as governors. The list follows: Thomas Jefferson, Governor of Virginia, 1779-81; James Monroe, Governor of Virginia, 1799-1802; Andrew Jackson, Governor of the Florida Territory, 1821; Martin Van Buren, Governor of New York, 1829; William Henry Harrison, Territorial Governor of Indiana, 1801-13; John Tyler, Governor of Virginia, 1825-26; James Knox Polk, Governor of Tennessee, 1839-41; Andrew Johnson, Governor of Tennessee, 1853-57, Military Governor of Tennessee, 1862-65; Rutherford Birchard Hayes, Governor of Ohio, 1868-72, Governor of Ohio, 1876-77; Grover Cleveland, Governor of New York, 1883-85; William McKinley, Governor of Ohio, 1892-96; Theodore Roosevelt, Governor of New York, 1898-1900; William Howard Taft, Governor of the Philippines, 1901-04; Woodrow Wilson, Governor of New Jersey, 1911-13; Calvin Coolidge, Governor of Massachusetts, 1919-20; Franklin Delano Roosevelt, Governor of New York, 1929-33; James Earl Carter, Jr., Governor of Georgia, 1971-75;

Ronald Wilson Reagan, Governor of California, 1967-75; William Jefferson Clinton, Governor of Arkansas, 1978-80, 1982-92; George Walker Bush, Governor of Texas, 1995-2000.

[vii] Article 1, Section 1, *U.S. Constitution*, 1787.

[viii] Article 2, Section 1, *U.S. Constitution*, 1787.

[ix] Amendment XXII, *U.S. Constitution*, 1787.

[x] 16th Amendment of the U.S. Constitution.

[xi] Thompson, Derek. "51% of Americans Pay No Federal Income Taxes." *The Atlantic* online. 4 May 2011. Date Accessed June 30, 2012.
http://www.theatlantic.com/business/archive/2011/05/51-of-americans-pay-no-federal-income-taxes/238329/

[xii] "Table 2.3.5 Personal Consumption Expenditures by Major Type of Product." Date Accessed 2/9/2012. US Department of Commerce Bureau of Economic Analysis.
http://www.bea.gov/iTable/iTable.cfm?ReqID=9&step=1

[xiii] U.S. Government Spending. "Time Series Chart of U.S. Government Spending." Date Accessed: 2.12.2012.
www.usgovernmentdebt.us/spending_chart_1792_2016USp_13s1li011mcn_H1f#copypaste.

[xiv] "National Debt." The Concord Coalition. 8 June 2012. Date Accessed June 30, 2012.
http://www.concordcoalition.org/issue-page/national-debt?gclid=CNL9qY2s27ECFYPrKgod-lcA1Q.

[xv] "Obama's 2012 Budget Proposals." *The Washington Post*. Date Accessed November, 2011.
www.washingtonpost.com/wp-srv/special/politics/documents/2012budget-full-historical.html.

[xvi] "Dilithium Crystals 'most likely' to power next generation." 18 June 2012. *Energy Bulletin*. Post Carbon Institute. Cambridge, Massachusetts. Date Accessed Jun 30, 2012. http://www.energybulletin.net/stories/2011-07-

11/americans-select-dilithium-crystals-power-next-generation

[xvii] "Energy Crisis 1970s." *The History Channel* Website. Date Accessed 3.7.2012.

[xviii] "The Energy Crisis and National Energy Policy Creation." Project on National Security Reform, Transforming Government for the 21st Century. Date Accessed, 3.7.2012.

[xix] Hollandsworth, Skip. "There will be boone." *Texas Monthly* Sept. 2008: 114+. *General OneFile* Web, 30 Oct. 2011.

[xx] Demographic Transition: An Historical Sociological Perspective. 2000. University of Michigan. Date Accessed: November 30, 2011. www.globalchange.umich.edu/globalchange2/current/lectures/pop_socio/pop_socio.html.

[xxi] "Arthur Brooks." American Enterprise Institute. Date Accessed: June 17, 2012. http://arthurbrooks.aei.org/about/about-arthur/.

[xxii] "The Social Security Act." *United States History* website. Online Highways. Date Accessed: March 18, 2012. http://www.u-s-history.com/pages/h1609.html.

[xxiii] Securities Act of 1933. http://www.sec.gov/about/laws/sa33.pdf.

[xxiv] Securities and Exchange Website. Date Accessed 3.21.2012.

[xxv] "Rebuilding the IPO On-Ramp: Putting Emerging Companies and the Job Market Back on the Road to Growth." P. 11. IPO Task Force, U.S. Treasury, October 20, 2011.

[xxvi]"Rebuilding the IPO On-Ramp: Putting Emerging Companies and the Job Market Back on the Road to Growth." IPO Task Force, US Treasury, October 20, 2011.

[xxvii] Ibid p. 13.

xxviii" Federal Deposit Insurance Corporation, Changes in Number of Institutions
FDIC-Insured Commercial Banks, United States and Other Areas, Year-to-Date Activity, 1984 – 2011. FDIC website, Industry Analysis, Bank Data and Statistics, Historical Statistics on Banking, Commercial Banks. Date Accessed 8.30.2012. http://www2.fdic.gov/hsob/HSOBRpt.asp. This downward trend continued in 2011, with 6291 banks.
xxix List of FDIC acts from other document.
xxx P.L. 106-102, 113 STAT 1338.
xxxi CNBC.com. "Wall Street Legend Sandy Weill: Break Up the Big Banks." 25 July 2012. Date Accessed August 1, 2012.
http://www.cnbc.com/id/48315170/Wall_Street_Legend_Sandy_Weill_Break_Up_the_Big_Banks
xxxiiCNBC.com. "Wall Street Legend Sandy Weill: Break Up the Big Banks." 25 July 2012. Date Accessed August 1, 2012.
http://www.cnbc.com/id/48315170/Wall_Street_Legend_Sandy_Weill_Break_Up_the_Big_Banks
xxxiii section 4 of the BHCA
xxxiv Federal Deposit Insurance Corporation, Number of Institutions, Branches and Total Offices FDIC Insured Commercial Banks United States and Other Areas, Balances at Year End, 1934-2011. Table CB01. Federal Deposit Insurance Corporation Website. Date Accessed 3.25.2012. http://www2.fdic.gov/hsob/HSOBRpt.asp.
xxxv Abu Dhabi Commercial Bank et al v. Morgan Stanley & Co et al, U.S. District Court, Southern District of New York, No. 08-07508; and King County, Washington et al v. IKB Deutsche Industriebank AG et al in the same court, No. 09-08387. http://www.crowell.com/PDF/Abu-Dhabi-Commercial-Bank_v_Morgan-Stanley.pdf
xxxvi Stempel, Jonathan. "NY judge won't dismiss lawsuits vs. Moody's, S&P." *Thomson Reuters Online*, "News &

Insight," May 7, 2012. Date accessed 5.24.2012.
http://newsandinsight.thomsonreuters.com/Legal/News/2
012/05_-
_May/NY_judge_won_t_dismiss_lawsuits_vs_Moody_s,_S
_P/

[xxxvii] Alvarez, Richard I and Mark J. Astarita, esq.
"Introduction to the Blue Sky Laws." Seclaw.com. Date
Accessed June 30, 2012.
http://www.seclaw.com/bluesky.htm

[xxxviii] "Regulation v. Deregulation." Date Accessed
2/13/2012. Apatheticvoter.com.
http://www.apatheticvoter.com/RegulationDeregulation.ht
m.

[xxxix] Source is the Bureau of Labor Statistics.

[xl] Frydman, Carola and Raven E. Saks. "Historical Trends in
Executive Compensation, 1936-2005." P. 66 Date
Accessed 08/23/2012.
http://www.vanderbilt.edu/econ/sempapers/Frydman1.pd
f.

[xli] "Official Declarations of War by Congress." *United States
Senate webpage.* Date Accessed 3/25/2012.
http://www.senate.gov/pagelayout/history/h_multi_sectio
ns_and_teasers/WarDeclarationsbyCongress.htm.

[xlii] "About Us: The Firm." Patriarch Partners website.
Date Accessed: 3.26.2012.
http://www.patriarchpartners.com/TheFirm.aspx.

[xliii] Tilton, Lynn. "It's Not Easy Being Blue." May 7, 2010.
Huff Post Business. Date Accessed 3/26/2012.
http://www.patriarchpartners.com/HerWritings.aspx .

[xliv] DeHaven, Tad. "Privatizing the U.S. Postal Service."
November 2010. The Cato Institute. March 26, 2012.
http://www.downsizinggovernment.org/print/usps.

[xlv] "James P. Cullen." Anderson Kill & Olick P.C. website.
Date accessed June 19, 2012.
http://www.andersonkill.com/attorneysprofile.asp?id=170

4. Helping and Hindering Disaster Relief Aid. The James and Mary Lassiter Distinguished Visiting Professor Conference. The University of Kentucky College of Law, November 4, 2011, Last updated March 5, 2012, Date Accessed June 19, 2012.
http://www.law.uky.edu/index.php?pid=387.

xlvi Cullen, Brigadier General James P. Cullen. "Standing Behind a Ban on Torture." The Huffington Post. January 27, 2009. Date Accessed June 19, 2012.
http://www.huffingtonpost.com/brigadier-general-james-p-cullen/standing-behind-a-ban-on_b_161314.html.

xlvii "An American Pastime: Smoking Pot." *Time Magazine*. Friday, Julyt 11, 2008. Date Accessed Jun 11, 2012.
http://www.time.com/time/health/article/0,8599,1821697,00.html.

xlviii Kesmodel, Desmond. "US Withdraws Labor Complaint Against Boeing." Wall Street Journal Online. December 10, 2011. Date Accessed: June 30, 2012.
http://online.wsj.com/article/SB10001424052970203413304577088374112815392.html#

xlix DeHaven, Tad. "Privatizing the U.S. Postal Service." November 2010. The Cato Institute. March 26, 2012.
http://www.downsizinggovernment.org/print/usps. Also, see Michael Crew and Paul Kleindorfer eds., *Competitive Transformation of the Postal and Delivery Sector* (Norwell, MA: Kluwer Academic Publishers, 2003).

l Bureau of Western Hemisphere Affairs. U.S. Relations with Haiti. U.S. Department of State. June 7, 2012. June 27, 2012. http://www.state.gov/r/pa/ei/bgn/1982.htm.

li Bureau of Western Hemisphere Affairs. U.S. Relations with Haiti. U.S. Department of State. June 7, 2012. June 27, 2012. http://www.state.gov/r/pa/ei/bgn/1982.htm

lii "Foreign Assistance Fast Facts." US Overseas Loans and Grants. USAID website. Date Accessed 4.1.2012. http://gbk.eads.usaidallnet.gov/data/fast-facts.html.

liii Ibid. These economies include Afghanistan, Haiti, Ethiopia, Kenya, and Tanzania.

liv Pakistan, Iraq, Sudan, Senegal, and West Bank/Gaza.

lv Colombia, Mexico, South Africa, Jordan, and Russia.

lvi Poland, Israel, Canada, Czech Republic, and Spain.

lvii "Brent Scowcroft." The Scowcroft Group website. Date Accessed June 19, 2012. http://www.scowcroft.com/html/staff/scowcroft.html.

lviii "Biography of Brent Scowcroft." United Nations Website. Date Accessed June 19, 2019. http://www.un.org/News/dh/hlpanel/scowcroft-bio.htm.

lix "Standard Country Report: Summary of All Countries, obligations in millions, constant 2010." U.S. Overseas Loans and Grants. USAID Foreign Assistant Data. Date Accessed 4.1.2012. http://gbk.eads.usaidallnet.gov/query/do.

lx "The Organic Act of the Department of Labor." The Department of Labor Timeline. Date Accessed 4.2.2012. http://www.dol.gov/oasam/programs/history/organact.htm.

lxi Taft, William Howard. Memorandum from President William Howard Taft. Memorandum to Accompany the Act to Create a Department of Labor. March 4, 1913. Date Accessed April 15, 2012. http://www.dol.gov/oasam/programs/history/memo.htm.

lxii Sullivan, Paul. "From Woman to Girl, an Introduction to Finance." *New York Times*. June 29, 2012. Date Accessed, June 29, 2012. http://www.nytimes.com/2012/06/30/your-money/investing-in-girls-gives-close-up-view-of-finance.html?pagewanted=1&_r=2&hp.

lxiii For more about the over-inflated sense of self-esteem, check out the following citation: "The Cult of Self-Esteem." *Atlantic Monthly*. 19 May 2010.

lxiv Henry, Peter. Minnesota English Journal. *The Case*

Against Standardized Testing. Accessed on July 3, 2012. http://www.mcte.org/journal/mej07/3Henry.pdf.

lxv Gates, Bill. How to keep America Competitive. Washington Post. February 25, 2007. Accessed July 5, 2012 from http://www.washingtonpost.com/wp-dyn/content/article/2007/02/23/AR2007022301697.html.
lxvi Kiladze, Tim. Why do Bill Gates and Google Love Salman Khan? The Globe and Mail. November 26, 2010. Accessed July 5, 2012 from http://www.theglobeandmail.com/report-on-business/rob-magazine/why-do-bill-gates-and-google-love-salman-khan/article1315626/
lxvii Martin, Jack & Eric A. Ruark. *The Fiscal Burden of Illegal Immigration on United States Taxpayers.* Federation for American Immigration Reform. February 2011.
lxviii Department of Homeland Security. Creation of the Department of Homeland Security. Last Reviewed June 6, 2011. June 27, 2012. http://www.dhs.gov/xabout/history/gc_1297963906741.shtm
lxix Napolitano, Janet. Quadrennial Homeland Security Review Report: A Strategic Framework for a Secure Homeland. Homeland Security. February 2010. June 27, 2012. http://www.dhs.gov/xlibrary/assets/qhsr_report.pdf.
lxx AOL Government. The Three Core Challenges Still Facing Homeland Security Department. AOL Inc. 2012. June 27, 2012.
lxxi Taft, William Howard. Memorandum from President William Howard Taft. Memorandum to Accompany the Act to Create a Department of Labor. March 4, 1913. Date Accessed April 15, 2012. http://www.dol.gov/oasam/programs/history/memo.htm.

lxxii "Saved Seed and Farmer Lawsuits." Monsanto Website. Date Accessed July 3, 2012. http://www.monsanto.com/newsviews/Pages/saved-seed-farmer-lawsuits.aspx.

lxxiii "300K farmers hope for lawsuit against Monsanto." February 15, 2012. Date Accessed July 3, 2012. http://rt.com/usa/news/farmers-monsanto-organic-farms-323/.

lxxiv Gillam, Carey. "Monsanto Lawsuit: Organic Farmers Appeal U.S. District Court Decision." Reuters via Huff Post Online. 03/28/2012. Date Accessed 07/04/2012. http://www.huffingtonpost.com/2012/03/28/monsanto-lawsuit-organic-farmers-appeal_n_1385693.html.

lxxv "Total USDA subsidies by state 2011." EWG Farm Subsidies. Date Accessed July 4, 2012. http://farm.ewg.org/progdetail.php?fips=00000&progcode=total&page=states&yr=2011&regionname=theUnitedStates

lxxvi "The United States Summary Information." EWG Farm Subsidies. Date Accessed July 5, 2012. http://farm.ewg.org/progdetail.php?fips=00000&progcode=total&page=states&yr=2011&regionname=theUnitedStates.